TO KEEP THE PEACE

TO
KEEP
THE
PEACE

The United Nations
Condemnatory Resolution

William W. Orbach

THE UNIVERSITY PRESS OF KENTUCKY

ISBN: 978-0-8131-5404-6

Library of Congress Catalog Card Number: 75–41989

Copyright © 1977 by The University Press of Kentucky

A statewide cooperative scholarly publishing agency
serving Berea College, Centre College of Kentucky,
Eastern Kentucky University, Georgetown College,
Kentucky Historical Society, Kentucky State University,
Morehead State University, Murray State University,
Northern Kentucky University, Transylvania University,
University of Kentucky, University of Louisville, and
Western Kentucky University.

Editorial and Sales Offices: Lexington, Kentucky 40506

To FIORELLA
WHO SUFFERED THROUGH ALL THIS

Contents

Preface

The primary function of the United Nations is to "maintain international peace and security, and to that end: to take effective collective measures for the prevention and removal of threats to the peace, and the suppression of acts of aggression" (UN Charter, Chapter I, Article 1). One of the primary means utilized by the United Nations to attain this end has been the condemnatory resolution.

In the pages that follow, I shall attempt to assess the development, reasons for, and effects of such resolutions in order to analyze the role of the United Nations at the present time.

I wish to make certain acknowledgments of deep gratitude for help in preparing this study. First, to Dr. Joseph Dunner, who encouraged and aided me in every possible way from my earliest undergraduate days. To Dr. John G. Stoessinger, whose advice in the preparation of this manuscript was invaluable. To Dr. Abraham Bargman, who spent countless hours with me analyzing and developing some of the ideas in this work. And finally, to my wife, who has selflessly supported me throughout, and without whose help I could never even have begun this manuscript. To her I owe all.

1

Introduction:
The Condemnatory Resolution

A resolution of collective delegitimization is a declaration by a group of states that the action of another state is not proper—that is, not in accord with the rules of international society. It is a statement by a recognized international body that the actions of a state are wrong, serving both as a judgment against that state and as a rebuke of it.

The concept of collective delegitimization is an outgrowth of the literature on legitimacy. Seymour M. Lipset gives perhaps the best definition of legitimacy: "the capacity of a system to engender and maintain the belief that the existing political institutions are the most appropriate ones for society." [1] However, this definition is really limited to the concept of *internal* legitimacy. Perhaps a more comprehensive definition of legitimacy, for the purposes of this work, should be based on the more common usage of the word—as correct, proper, or just—that is, in accordance with the rules and traditions of the particular society in question. Legitimacy, internal or external, could thus be defined as the belief of a society's members that an action, policy, or government is in accord with the rules and traditions of that society.

Internal legitimacy is essential for the continued existence of any government. The failure of a government to gain legitimacy in the eyes of its people will undermine it and make it susceptible to revolution. External legitimacy is not as essential to the continued viability of the state; it is conceivable that a government or state survive without it. Thus, one state can declare the policies or actions of another state's government somehow illegitimate without threatening that state's existence. This is delegitimization. When a *group* of states declares that a policy or action of a state's government is not in accord with the commonly accepted rules and regulations of the international arena, the process is called *collective delegitimization.*[2]

Delegitimizations must be based on some standard. In order to declare that the policy (or government) of a state is not in accord with certain rules, one must first identify those rules. Standards for internal legitimacy are not difficult to find. They are a nation's constitution, written or unwritten, together with its customs, habits, mores, and traditions. A government is illegitimate if it fails to act in accord with the principles of that society. Standards for external legitimacy are more difficult to establish. International law is neither universally accepted nor obeyed, although international treaties have certainly provided some standard; and since the legitimacy of a government's policies or actions in the eyes of other states will depend on their accord with the moral principles and beliefs of the legitimizers, the importance of international customs and mores cannot be ignored. That is, Communist states are more likely to legitimize other Communist states, and democracies, other democracies, and so on.

With the advent of the United Nations this rather vague and arbitrary system of standards was formalized. The UN Charter became the basis for a collective determination of the legitimacy of the policies, actions, or governments of states. Policies or actions in accord with the Charter or with UN resolutions based upon the Charter are considered legitimate; other policies and actions are declared illegitimate. Thus, South Africa has been condemned for its policy of *apartheid* because it contradicts the Charter principles reaffirming the equality of all men and their right to self-determination. And the People's Republic of China was condemned for its action in Korea because it violated the Charter injunction against aggression.

The United Nations is not a legal institution, however, and the Charter has not established a legal standard for collective delegitimization. UN standards are actually a unique mixture of both the political situation and the moral standards operative in the international arena at any given time. In other words, the United Nations is not an impartial organization objectively assessing and considering each international conflict as it arises, but a political body reflecting the interests of its membership. The selection of issues is based on subjective, not objective grounds. So the United Nations is neither an arbiter of international law, nor the moral conscience of mankind, but a convenient international forum in which a state can discern the policies and opinions of its fellow states and make known its own.

It will become apparent here that in many cases, the question of how many approved the resolution is less essential than *who* approved it, and the debate may be more carefully studied (to ascertain the positions of participants and nonparticipants) than the actual wording of the resolution itself. This is why one can question Inis L. Claude's assertion that statesmen "are keenly conscious of the need for approval by as large and impressive a body of other states as may be possible, for multilateral endorsement of their position." [3] Do they seek UN approval for its intrinsic value—or because it represents the policies of individual states? Do they cherish collective legitimization as a unique entity—or because within it are contained the individual legitimizations of their friends and allies? These questions assume, of course, that states vote in the United Nations according to their own interests. But how in fact does one determine whether votes in the United Nations actually reflect the national interests and policies of the member states, or whether these states are merely engaged in a grotesque propaganda charade? In other words, is the whole UN procedure a serious exercise in decision-making, or a diplomatic game? Do the states believe that their resolutions will be of any consequence outside the immediate vicinity of Turtle Bay?

One counters such questions with others: If UN procedure is little more than a game, how can one explain the great effort on the part of member states to have some resolutions passed and others defeated? If resolutions mean so little, why do the Soviets consistently veto them? How can one account for the West's reluctance to have anticolonial resolutions passed; or the United Kingdom's eagerness both for resolutions supporting its policy in Rhodesia and vetoes of resolutions advocating force against that state? Indeed, why would the states so insist upon retaining the veto if resolutions don't mean anything anyway? Why was there so much effort to have the People's Republic of China admitted to or kept out of the United Nations if membership reflects nothing?

Whether UN resolutions actually accomplish anything seems immaterial so long as states believe that they do. It is important to realize that a resolution of collective delegitimization is generally a combination of *two* factors: it is, first, a joint declaration by a group of states that their own actions toward the object state *are* in accord with international law and authorized to continue in the future, and *second,* a declaration that the object state's policies or actions are not. Such a collective legitimization has its beneficial effects, and even those states that do not actually require this approval may want it. In the case of collective legitimization the number of states supporting a resolution is indeed more important than the respective positions of the individual supporters. A near-unanimous vote on a resolution declaring the supporters' action legitimate is more desirable than a bare majority, even should this majority include the states allied with the object state. This is one reason why African and Arab states have consistently sought collective delegitimization of their foes. The massive legitimization of their own position entailed by a resolution that collectively delegitimizes their foes cannot fail to benefit them, if only to massage their egos.

In the case of collective delegitimization of an object state, the situation is different; when a majority of UN members judges that certain actions or policies of a state are wrong, the positions of individual states within that majority become important. A state will not be concerned if only its foes vote to delegitimize its government or policies while neutral states and allies vote against the resolution or abstain. Every object state has had a hard core of opponents allied against it, and a resolution supported by these states and no others is of little consequence. Only when an object state's foes gain the support of neutrals, or worse, that state's allies does it have reason to be concerned. The reasons for this are basic. Although an object state's allies will not be as concerned as the object state itself about the continued viability of its government, their attitude is certainly favorable, and they will generally not support a policy designed to destroy that government. No state can afford to be completely isolated in today's interdependent world; no state is self-sufficient. Even if a state could conceivably survive in isolation, it would be on a considerably lowered standard of living, and no state wants to be put in this position. Once a state's friends support a resolution of collective delegitimization against them they face international isolation and are likely to consider compromise. Thus, although the number of votes for a resolution of collective delegitimization is important, in this case, the source of those votes is the essential factor.

The situation is complicated, however, by the tendency of states to vote against their short-term interests in order to safeguard their longer term interests, or in favor of "morality." For example, the United States would certainly prefer not to condemn South Africa or Portugal, but fearing a loss of influence among the African states, it has joined in the condemnations (though it has drawn the line when measures are suggested to enforce these resolutions).

So, while UN resolutions are not simply the products of a frivolous diplomatic game, they are nevertheless a distorted mirror on reality, and this diminishes their utility. Many African states are actually weakening the United Nations by pressuring states to take a "moral" position and support resolutions they do not truly endorse. Since the United Nations is basically a political institution, such resolutions actually have little moral validity; yet just enough moral pressure is injected into the proceedings to cloud the real positions of member states. Thus, such resolutions are neither a consistent moral nor an accurate political reflector. This emasculates the United Nations in two ways: first, the prestige of the institution is eroded by the passage of meaningless resolutions that have little or no chance of implementation; second, collective delegitimization cannot serve its function when states depart from the assertion of their selfish, but actual, foreign policy into the high-sounding, but hypocritical realm of "true morality and justice." [4]

To be fair, collective delegitimizations are generally expressed by way of condemnatory resolutions, and part of the problem lies with the resolution itself. For the most part, a resolution is the final result of, or decision reached through a debate in the General Assembly or Security Council. Ideally it represents the consensus of the participants in the debate—but more often than not it is the product of conflict and some compromise. Because most political blocs do not have the necessary majority of votes to pass resolutions in their own interests, the support of other blocs is essential. This support can be gained only through compromise. Also, even if a group has a majority of votes in the General Assembly—as does the Afro-Asian bloc—it will still attempt to gain support from other blocs so as to have a near-unanimous vote on resolutions of interest to it. It will especially seek the support of the friends and allies of the state being condemned.

The passage of a resolution is similar in this way to the passage of a bill through a domestic parliament; but whereas a domestic parliament's authority is clear, the authority of an international resolution depends generally upon four factors:

(1) *The body passing the resolution.* General Assembly resolutions simply recommend, and in most cases these resolutions are not binding. (The exceptions are budgetary, election, membership, and instructive resolutions to the Secretary General.) Security Council resolutions, on the other hand, are binding if based on Chapter VII of the Charter; however, the present international situation makes the great majority of them well-nigh unenforceable.

(2) *The majority by which the resolution is passed.* A resolution that is passed by a unanimous or near-unanimous vote has far more moral authority than one passed by a simple majority. In addition, the position of various states on a resolution provides a clue to the resolution's importance as well as to its chances for implementation.

(3) *The topic of the resolution.* Some resolutions are devoted to issues about which there is little or no conflict and merely express the consensus of the organization. For example, resolutions admitting new states to membership in the United Nations have been routinely implemented in the last decade and a half. Other resolutions are approved only after long and vociferous debate. The efficacy of such resolutions depends upon the intensity of the resolve on both sides. Thus the resolutions

calling for aid to South Korea in the Korean conflict were implemented; resolutions directed against South Africa were not.

(4) *The type of action recommended.* The resolution may recommend continuation of the present policy of a state or organization or it may recommend changes. Proposals for change generally have less chance for implementation than do requests for continuation. The possibilities for implementation vary even within proposals for change according to the extent of change requested.

According to the more general definition, a condemnatory resolution is *any* resolution directed against the policies, actions, or government of a state. The problem with this definition is that it includes cases of collective disapproval and this is too broad an area for effective analysis. The more technical and limited definition of condemnation is confined to resolutions that expressly utilize the word "condemns" or "censures," or accuse a state of aggression. Certain conventions in wording and construction make clear the intensity of such resolutions:

Although a condemnatory resolution is usually introduced either by the word "condemns" or the word "censures," the terms are by no means identical. "Condemns" is the strongest verbal action that the United Nations can take (with the exception of a declaration of aggression) and was used infrequently and with great caution in the first decade and a half of the organization's history. "Censures" is used when the members of the United Nations hesitate to use the word "condemns" against a state, yet believe that a term of disapproval is too weak for purposes of rebuke. For example, in November 1953 the United Nations wished to reprove Israel for its raid on Kibya, yet felt the use of the word "condemns" would be too severe a blow to the young state. "Censures" was therefore adopted as a compromise.

The position of the condemnation clause in the resolution as a whole is crucial. UN resolutions are generally divided into two distinct sections: the preamble and the operative paragraphs. The preamble is a descriptive introduction to the resolution; it is passive. The operative paragraphs cover the recommendations or decisions in detail and are the active part of the resolution. Therefore, a condemnation in the operative paragraphs is far more serious than one in the preamble.

The target of the condemnation may vary. The condemnation may be directed against the state itself or against its policies or actions. The latter is far less severe, and the United Nations prefers it because it allows more flexibility both for the United Nations and for all states concerned.

The name of the state condemned may be implicit or explicit in a resolution of condemnation. The state may be named in the condemnatory clause itself; it may be named in the resolution but not in the clause; or it may not be named at all, although the object of the resolution is known to all. The severity of the resolution of condemnation declines in direct proportion to its lack of specificity.

The resolution may actually pronounce a condemnation or it may merely reaffirm a previous resolution of condemnation. The fact that the United Nations has decided not to condemn a state anew but merely to reaffirm a previous condemnation decreases the severity of the present resolution.

In addition to these variations a resolution may use one or several terms of condemnation at the same time or may intersperse phrases of disapproval with phrases of condemnation in a single resolution. Even if these additional phrases of condemnation or disapproval are not directed against the state itself but against its allies or trading partners, each term nevertheless increases the severity of the resolution as a whole.

A condemnation, then, according to this more restricted definition, is significantly more than strong disapproval. Anyone can disapprove of a policy, but one who has the power to *judge* becomes the arbiter of right and wrong. Thus the United Nations is the arbiter of international right and wrong—a significant power. This power is the crux of collective legitimization or delegitimization, and is the moral foundation for the United Nations.

Assuming then that the United Nations has become the dispenser of legitimacy in the international arena, what is the basis in the United Nations Charter for the power of collective delegitimization? The answer depends upon what collective delegitimization is actually intended to be—a prelude to further action, a substitute for any action, or a form of action itself. If it is a prelude to enforcement action, then the entire concept is included in Article 39 (Chapter VIII) of the Charter:

> The Security Council shall determine the existence of any threat to the peace, breach of the peace, or act of aggression and shall make recommendations, or decide what measures shall be taken in accordance with Articles 41 and 42, to maintain or restore international peace and security.

In such a case pressure is exerted to collectively delegitimize a state in the hope that a resolution so passed will enable the United Nations to take further action under Chapter VII. Article 39 establishes the legality of such a resolution only on the part of the Security Council, however; the basis for such a resolution in the General Assembly is not to be found in the Charter at all, but in the Uniting for Peace resolution [377 (V)] of November 3, 1950.

> The General Assembly . . . Resolves that if the Security Council, because of lack of unanimity of the permanent members, fails to exercise its primary responsibility for the maintenance of international peace and security in any case where there appears to be a threat to the peace, or act of aggression, the General Assembly shall consider the matter immediately with a view to making appropriate recommendations to Members for collective measures, including in the case of a breach of the peace or act of aggression the use of armed force when necessary, to maintain or restore international peace and security.

Once the General Assembly can recommend collective measures, it can also collectively delegitimize the policy or action of a state guilty of wrongdoing, thus paving the way, morally if not legally, for taking collective measures.

On the other hand, many resolutions of collective delegitimization are merely a substitute for, not a prelude to, action. Although the sponsors may hope that their resolution will lead to enforcement action, many states vote for it in order to increase their prestige in the eyes of the sponsoring and supporting states, or to relieve pressure placed on them, or because they are not willing to allow the United Nations to take further action. Even the sponsors often realize that no action against the guilty state is possible at the time and press for these resolutions as an expression of their determination to do *something,* as well as to satisfy domestic critics clamoring for action. Although native guerrillas have now succeeded in taking effective military action in Portugal, resolutions collectively delegitimizing both Portugal and South Africa have reflected the under- standing of many African states that the United Nations cannot take effective military action; this is why they have resorted to resolutions.

As a substitute for action, resolutions of collective delegiti- mization can be included within the scope of Articles 10–14 (Chapter IV) and Chapter VI—especially Article 37—of the UN Charter. Article 37 states:

> 1. Should the parties to a dispute of the nature referred to in Article 33 fail to settle it by the means indicated in that Article, they shall refer it to the Security Council.
> 2. If the Security Council deems that the continuance of the dispute is in fact likely to endanger the maintenance of international peace and security, it shall decide whether to take action under Article 36 or to recommend such terms of settlement as it may consider appropriate.

Thus the Security Council has the power of recommendation in any dispute threatening to undermine international peace.

Articles 10–14 (Chapter IV) give even broader powers of recommendation to the General Assembly by allowing it to discuss any subject covered in the Charter, not merely matters threatening international peace and security.

> The General Assembly may discuss any questions or any matters within the scope of the present Charter or relating to the powers and functions of any organs provided for in the present Charter and, except as provided in Article 12, may make recommendations to the Members of the United Na- tions or to the Security Council or to both on any such ques- tions or matters. (Article 10)

> The General Assembly may discuss any questions relating to the maintenance of international peace and security brought before it by any Member of the United Nations, or by the Security Council, or by a state which is not a

Member of the United Nations in accordance with Article 35, paragraph 2, and may make recommendations with regard to any such questions to the state or states concerned or to the Security Council or to both. (Article 11)

The General Assembly may recommend measures for the peaceful adjustment of any situation, regardless of origin, which it deems likely to impair the general welfare or friendly relations among nations, including situations resulting from a violation of the provisions of the present Charter. (Article 14)

Since the General Assembly can make recommendations in situations resulting from a violation of the principles of the Charter as outlined in Chapter I, it can discuss aggression and the self-determination of peoples.

Thus, both the General Assembly and the Security Council clearly have the power to recommend in such cases—and prerequisite to any recommendation, the ability to judge the policies or actions of a state. So if collective delegitimization is merely a substitute for action, then the power is included in the power of recommendation.

Collective delegitimization may also be a form of nonmilitary sanction that the United Nations can utilize to enforce its decisions. Although it is less potent than economic or diplomatic sanctions, it is nevertheless a sanction. The basis for this power is to be found in Article 41 (Chapter VII) of the UN Charter:

The Security Council may decide what measures not involving the use of armed force are to be employed to give effect to its decisions, and it may call upon the Members of the United Nations to apply such measures. These may include complete or partial interruption of economic relations and of rail, air, sea, postal, telegraphic, radio, and other means of communication, and the severance of diplomatic relations.

Though not expressly stated, moral condemnations could be included under this article.

Again, the legality of such resolutions of collective delegitimization in the Security Council is clear. With the General Assembly the situation is different. One can claim that the Uniting for Peace resolution gives the General Assembly the power to recommend collective measures, leaving the states to implement them voluntarily. But unlike economic, diplomatic, or military sanctions, which are simply recommended and can be implemented or not implemented as the member states desire, the very nature of a collective delegitimization resolution requires no further action from the member states; it is an action in itself. Thus, since the General Assembly cannot itself take action, any resolutions of collective delegitimization which are enacted by the General Assembly are of doubtful legality.

The legal problem becomes more relevant when we consider the fact that the judgmental aspect is only part of a condemnation. Most condemnatory resolutions as a whole are divided into two sectors: the negative or condemning sector and the positive or suggestive sector. Many go beyond condemnation and request either a change in policy or the adoption of an entirely new policy. For example:

> The General Assembly . . . Condemns the trial of the eight Namibians under the Terrorism Act which took place at Windhoek between July and November 1969, and further calls upon the government of South Africa:
> (a) To release immediately and unconditionally those tried under the above-mentioned Terrorist Act;
> (b) To desist forthwith from the extension of the "Bantusan" system into Namibia.[5]

What, then, does the United Nations expect to accomplish by condemning a state? Apparently, it hopes that the condemned state will alter its objectionable policy and follow UN directives. In fact, the United Nations will often threaten further measures if its directives are not obeyed:

> The Security Council . . . Condemns the failure of Israel to comply with the aforementioned resolutions and calls upon it to implement forthwith the provisions of these resolutions. . . .
> Reiterates the determination . . . that, in the event of a negative response or no response, the Security Council shall convene without delay to consider what further action should be taken in this matter.[6]

But a policy forcibly imposed is a *command,* not a recommendation. Obviously, the legality of such resolutions, if passed by the General Assembly, is open to question. The power to condemn is in accord with the Charter, but the power to command a state to alter its actions, policies, or government on pain of further condemnation is not.

A similar problem is raised when one considers the actions or policies for which states are condemned. There are two basic reasons for a UN condemnation: refusal to heed the Charter or refusal to heed previous resolutions. Yet when the General Assembly condemns a state for not heeding its resolutions, it is delegating to itself powers not granted in the Charter. The implication of such condemnations is that the previous resolutions are mandatory—how else could a state be condemned for not heeding them? Thus by issuing these recommendations the General Assembly is itself violating the UN Charter.

This point raises an important question. A condemnatory resolution, if confined to its rhetorical effects, has, by its very passage, legitimized one side of a conflict and delegitimized the other. But when a resolution is no longer self-implementing, what factors will influence a state to change its offending policies? We return again to collective versus individual delegitimization. When resolutions of collective delegitimization are rhetorically self-implementing, their collective nature is most important: the more numerous the supporters of a collective delegitimization, the more its rhetorical action becomes a world action. But the effects of a resolution on *policy* depend upon which states favor the resolution. Individual, not collective, delegitimizations are the key to policy change.

On the other hand, were it not for the practice of collective delegitimization in the United Nations, there would be few individual delegitimizations. If states were not forced to take a stand on international conflicts, few states would criticize the policies of their friends and allies. So collective delegitimization releases the potent powers of individual delegitimizations.

Collective delegitimizations also induce further international pressure on the object state. Witness South Africa's exclusion from the Olympic Games and withdrawal from the Common-

Total United Nations Condemnations, 1946 - 1974

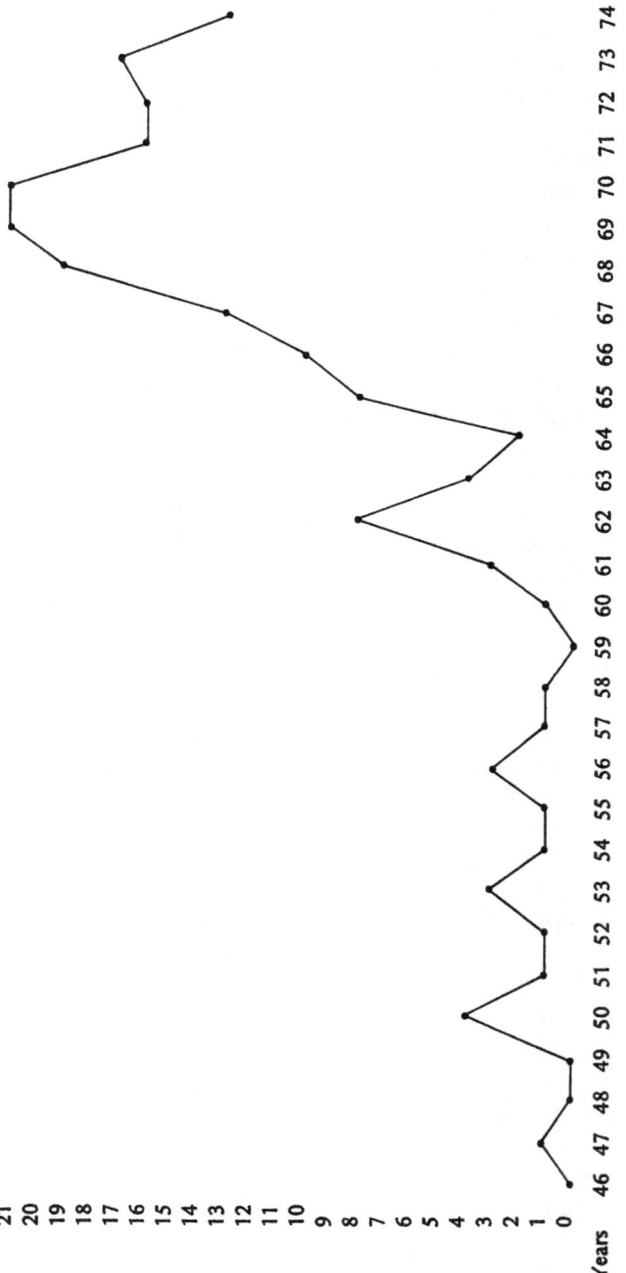

Number of
condemnations

Years

wealth, the International Labor Organization, and the Food and Agriculture Organization.

The process of collective delegitimization at the United Nations can become a symbol for general world delegitimization as well as a cause. In turn, world action and reaction forces the allies and friends of a state to take a further stand, leading to still more pressures on the object state to alter the policies or actions in question.

Collective delegitimization, then, creates both individual delegitimizations of the condemned state by its allies and friends, and at the same time is dependent upon them for rhetorical success. Yet the collective nature of the United Nations has changed very much over the three decades of its existence, and the types and quantity of resolutions passed pre- and post-1960 reflect the great shift in regional and political membership in the organization. Consideration of this situation can give us some insight into the strengths and limitations of the United Nations as an organization, as it reveals the gradual evolution of the condemnatory resolution as an international tool.

Until 1960, General Assembly resolutions were used by the West to condemn the Soviet Union and Communist bloc states. However, these condemnatory resolutions were a minute portion of all General Assembly resolutions of that period. From 1946 to 1960 there were 1,577 resolutions, only fourteen of which were condemnatory resolutions. So during the first fourteen years of UN existence, the General Assembly passed an average of one condemnatory resolution a year, or approximately one out of every 112 resolutions.

In the decade that followed, both the emphasis and the number of condemnations changed dramatically. Few, if any, North–South issues in the pre-1960 period led to a condemnation, although the Indonesian case came close. During the 1960s North–South issues became the *focus* of condemnations, and there were no further condemnations of Communist states. South Africa was condemned for its internal policy of *apartheid* and for its refusal to grant South-West Africa independence; Portugal was condemned for its continuing policy of colonialism in Africa, primarily in Angola, Mozambique, and

Portuguese Guinea; and Southern Rhodesia (and indirectly the United Kingdom) was condemned for its unilateral declaration of independence and refusal to grant majority rule. So great was the shift of emphasis that the West was now condemned for its alleged support of the remaining white-dominated or colonialist states in Africa. The numerical change has been equally striking. In the years 1960–1973 there were 113 condemnations out of 2,001 resolutions, an average of over eight condemnations per year, or approximately one for every eighteen General Assembly resolutions.

The pattern in the Security Council has not been the same, because both East and West have built-in vetoes. Since resolutions can be approved only with the overt or tacit consent of the five permanent powers, it is logical to assume that the states which have been condemned lack their support, or that these powers find it more in their interest not to veto a condemnatory resolution than to do so. As a matter of fact, until 1964 Israel was the only state consistently condemned by the Security Council, its actions alienating even its friends.

From 1946 to 1964 the Security Council passed five condemnatory resolutions out of a total of 185, an average of one condemnation every 4½ years or every 37 resolutions. Since 1964, however, the Security Council has rapidly increased the rate and scope of its condemnations. (Even the United Kingdom was condemned by the Security Council, albeit indirectly, in its consideration of the reprisals against Yemen.) The number of condemnations swelled to 40 out of 159 Security Council resolutions from 1964 till 1973. Twenty-five percent of all resolutions were condemnations, or four each year, in contrast to the period till 1964 when only 2 percent of Security Council resolutions were condemnations. In the first decade and a half of its existence the United Nations approved seventeen condemnations out of 1,762 resolutions, an average of more than one a year, or one in every 103.5 resolutions. From 1960 to 1973 the United Nations passed 155 condemnatory resolutions out of a total of 2,213 resolutions, averaging eleven a year, or approximately one in every fourteen resolutions. The years 1964–1973 show an even more dramatic rate of increase. In this period there were 139 condemnatory resolutions out of a total of 1,338 resolutions—a rate of approximately fourteen a year, or nearly one in every ten resolutions.

One of the reasons for this dramatic increase in the number of condemnations since 1960 is the rapid increase in UN membership in recent years. From 1946 to 1973 UN membership more than doubled, increasing from 51 to 135 states. This growth was not evenly distributed among the regional blocs. Also, geographical location does not ensure political ties within that region. Table 1 illustrates UN growth by regional blocs, making note of those states that vote as a political bloc with states outside of their respective regional blocs. Thus, over the past three decades, the Latin American, Western European/North American, and Eastern European groups declined in percentage of votes in the General Assembly, while the African, Asian, and Arab groups increased their voting power. The Latin American group had the smallest gain in membership, merely five new states. In 1945 this group controlled 29 percent of the General Assembly votes; by 1973 it controlled only 18.5 percent, despite the gain in membership. The Western European/North American group had an increase in membership from thirteen to 23 states, but decreased in voting power from 25.5 percent to 17 percent. The Soviet group nearly doubled its membership, but it too lost in voting power. In 1945 it consisted of six states, controlling nearly 12 percent of the total votes; in 1973 its eleven member states held only 8 percent of the votes in the General Assembly.

The underdeveloped groups were the major gainers in General Assembly membership over the past three decades. The Arab group grew from five states, controlling nearly 10 percent of the total vote in 1945, to eighteen states, controlling 13 percent in 1973. The Asian group gained in membership by 26 states, going from eight states, or almost 16 percent of the total vote in 1945, to 34, or 25 percent in 1973. Finally, the African group consisted of only four states, controlling almost 8 percent in 1945; in 1973 it had 42 members, or 31 percent of the vote.

It is apparent that the changing character of UN membership over the past 30 years parallels the pattern of changing interests over the same period. When membership was limited to states

TABLE 1
Regional and Political Alignment in the General Assembly, 1945-1973

Year	Eastern European region	Year	Western European/ N. American region	Year	Latin American region	Year	Asian region	Year	African region
1945	Byelorussia	1945	Australia*	1945	Argentina	1945	China†	1945	Egypt‡
	Czechoslovakia		Belgium		Bolivia		India*		Ethiopia
	Poland		Canada*		Brazil		Iran		Liberia
	Ukraine		Denmark		Chile		Iraq†		S. Africa†
	USSR		France		Colombia		Lebanon‡	1955	Libya‡
	Yugoslavia†		Greece		Costa Rica		Philippines	1956	Morocco‡
1955	Albania		Luxembourg		Cuba		Saudi Arabia‡		Sudan‡
	Bulgaria		Netherlands		Dominican Rep.		Syria‡		Tunisia‡
	Hungary		New Zealand*		Ecuador	1946	Afghanistan	1957	Ghana*
	Romania		Norway		El Salvador		Thailand	1958	Guinea
			Turkey		Guatemala	1947	Pakistan*		
			United Kingdom*		Haiti		Yemen‡		
		1946	Iceland		Honduras	1948	Burma		
			Sweden		Mexico	1949	Israel		
		1955	Austria		Nicaragua	1950	Indonesia		
			Finland		Panama	1955	Cambodia		
			Ireland		Paraguay		Ceylon*		
			Italy		Peru		Jordan‡		
			Portugal		Uruguay		Laos		
			Spain		Venezuela		Nepal		
						1956	Japan		
						1957	Malaya*		

Year	Country
1973	German Dem. Rep.
1964	Malta
1973	Fed. Rep. of Germany

Year	Country
1962	Jamaica*
	Trinidad & Tobago*
1966	Barbados*
1973	Guyana*
	Bahamas*

Year	Country
1960	Cyprus*
1961	Mongolia
1963	Kuwait‡
1965	Maldiv Isl.
	Singapore
	-Indonesia*
1966	Indonesia
1967	S. Yemen‡
1970	Fiji*
1971	Bhutan‡
	Bahrain‡
	Qatar‡
	Oman‡
	United Arab‡
	Emirates‡

Year	Country
1960	Cameroon
	Central Afr. Rep
	Chad
	Congo
	Dahomey
	Gabon
	Ivory Coast
	Madagascar
	Mali
	Niger
	Nigeria*
	Senegal
	Somalia
	Togo
	Upper Volta
	Zaire
1961	Mauritania*
	Sierre Leone*
	Tanganyika*
1962	Algeria‡
	Burundi‡
	Rwanda‡
	Uganda*
1963	Kenya*
	Zanzibar*
1964	Malawi*
	Zambia*
1965	Gambia*
1966	Botswana*
	Lesotho*
1968	Equat. Guinea*
	Mauritius*
	Swaziland*

*Politically tied with Commonwealth bloc
†Nonaligned
‡Politically tied with Arab bloc (plus Syria in 1961)

whose major concern was the East–West struggle, UN condemnations were confined to that sphere. With the dramatic rise in states whose major concern was the North–South struggle, UN interest and condemnations shifted to that sphere.

This conclusion is borne out further if the sponsors of the condemnatory resolutions, the abstentions, and negative votes from 1945 to 1960 are listed by regional groups (Table 2). Clearly, the vast majority of states sponsoring pre-1960 condemnatory resolutions were Western or pro-Western states. And most of the above resolutions were directed explicitly against the Soviet bloc: resolution 385 condemned Bulgaria, Hungary, and Romania for violating human rights; resolution 498 accused China of aggression; resolution 618 condemned Albania, Bulgaria, Czechoslovakia, Hungary, Poland, and Romania for their refusal to repatriate Greek children; resolution 906 condemned North Korea and the People's Republic of China for the detention of UN prisoners of war; and resolutions 1004, 1133, and 1312 condemned the Soviet Union for its invasion of Hungary. Other resolutions (380, 381) indirectly condemned the Soviet bloc. The Soviet Union was vigorous in its protest against both types.

In short, the West sponsored and supported resolutions condemning the East; the East strongly objected and attempted to block their passage. Since the West was numerically dominant in this period, it had little difficulty winning approval for these resolutions. Despite this fact, resolutions of condemnation were relatively rare during this period.

Resolutions of condemnation approved since 1960 present a radical change in perspective. For one thing, the vast majority of those states that have sponsored post-1960 condemnatory resolutions are not original UN members, and nearly half were themselves admitted after 1960. More important, when the sponsors are broken down into regional groups, the following facts become apparent: (1) The vast majority, generally over 90 percent of those sponsoring resolutions of condemnation in the General Assembly, are members of either the African or the Asian group. (2) Within the ranks of those sponsoring condemnatory resolutions the Africans outnumber the Asians two to one. In many cases nearly 75 percent of all African members

TABLE 2

Sponsors, Abstentions, and Negative Votes
for General Assembly Condemnatory Resolutions,
by Region, 1945-1960

Condemnatory res. no.	Eastern European region			Western European/ North American region			Latin American region			Asian region			African region		
	sponsored	abstained	negative	sponsored	abstained	negative	sponsored	abstained	negative	sponsored	abstained	negative	sponsored	abstained	negative
380	0	1	5	4	0	0	2	0	0	2	0	0	0	0	0
381	0	1	5	0	0	0	1	0	0	0	0	0	0	0	0
385	0	1	5	1	0	0	0	0	0	0	*	0	0	*	0
498	0	1	5	1	0	0	0	0	0	0	5	2	0	1	0
618	0	1	5	1	0	0	1	0	0	0	5	0	0	0	0
906	0	1	5	1	0	0	0	0	0	0	5	0	0	0	0
1004	0	1	8	1	1†	0	0	0	0	0	11	0	0	2	0
1133	0	0	10	15	1†	0	18	0	0	3	8	0	1	1	0
1312	0	0	10	15	2†	0	17	0	0	5	7	0	0	6	0

*Information not available
†Finland

in the United Nations sponsor these resolutions, whereas approximately 50 percent of the Asian group, which has fewer members than the African group, tends to do so. (3) Few members of the Latin American and Eastern European groups, with the exception of Yugoslavia, have sponsored condemnatory resolutions since 1960. (4) Members of the Western European group have rarely sponsored post-1960 condemnatory resolutions. Generally speaking, most of these resolutions have been aimed, at least indirectly, against the interests of the Western European states.

Thus, sponsorship of post-1960 condemnatory resolutions can be ranked, in the order of most to least participation, as follows:

African, Asian, Latin American, Eastern European, and Western European.

The lines of demarcation in voting are not altogether precise because unless a resolution is totally unrealistic or obviously aimed against a state's own interests, most states, including those from the West, will generally acquiesce to the will of the majority and vote for the resolution to avoid offending the uncommitted states. However, a state may indicate its displeasure by abstaining rather than voting for or against a resolution. It is therefore useful to study abstentions as well as the more obvious negative votes on condemnatory resolutions. Several facts emerge from such a study:

The vast majority of states that have abstained or voted against post-1960 condemnatory resolutions are either original members of the United Nations or were admitted before 1960. Few, if any, states who were admitted after 1960 abstain from, and practically none vote against, condemnatory resolutions. When these abstentions and negative votes are examined in terms of regional groups, it becomes clear that (1) with the exception of the Republic of South Africa,[7] most African states support condemnatory resolutions, as do most Asian states. Few abstain on these resolutions and even fewer vote against them. (2) In general, the Eastern European group strongly supports condemnatory resolutions, although these states often charge that the resolutions are too weak. (3) Most Latin American states vote for condemnatory resolutions; a few sometimes abstain. Only in rare instances does a Latin American state vote against one of these resolutions. (4) A large proportion (usually over 75 percent) of those abstaining or voting against these condemnatory resolutions are Western European states or their allies.

The few African states that did abstain on condemnatory resolutions affecting South Africa were generally economically dependent on or hoped to gain economic benefits from South Africa. However, some African states have lately abstained on condemnatory resolutions, their leaders asserting that since force seems to accomplish nothing, perhaps a dialogue with South Africa would serve to change the state's policy.

There are certain elements common to General Assembly

condemnatory resolutions or their targets that must be considered. Each of the condemned states has a determined group of states allied against it, bound together by the belief that the continued existence of the condemned state in its present form is a threat to the very principles upon which they were founded. They are hostile, afraid, determined to effect a drastic alteration of the condemned state's policies, or destruction of the state itself. When the Western states considered the Soviet Union and its allies a mortal danger in the 1950s, they wished to limit the expansion of those states; the Arab states hate and fear Israel and wish to destroy it; the African states hate and fear South Africa, Southern Rhodesia, and the Portuguese policy of colonialism and wish to be rid of them. In 1960, sixteen African states were admitted to the United Nations, increasing that bloc's size from ten to 26 members; in the following year the United Nations condemned both South Africa and Portugal for the first time, and the number of condemnations tripled. Although this is no direct proof that one factor has any connection with the other, in light of the previous point it may be considered circumstantial evidence, especially if one also takes into account the fact that the African states had both motive and opportunity.

In the Security Council, most condemnatory resolutions are passed in response to a crisis rather than to an ongoing situation. The Security Council was formed in order to deal with crises and therefore has a small membership and the permanent presence of the five major powers (as well as their vetoes should they ever come into conflict). Since efficient and immediate action in a crisis necessitates a small body, the Security Council, until 1966, was composed of only eleven members, an additional four being added in that year. One would therefore not expect the African group to have an excessive influence on that body. Yet the fact is that the African group, sometimes in combination with the Asian group, wields great influence in the Security Council. There are several reasons for this:

First, the African group has had at least two votes in the Security Council each year since 1961, with the exception of 1965. Before this period it usually had no votes, or at best one; Egypt was a member for three years, Tunisia for two years.

But neither of these states was truly African in terms of its interests at the time. The occasional lone African vote pre-1961 was one-eleventh, or a little more than 9 percent of the total voting power in the Security Council. Since 1961 the African group has had at least two-elevenths, or just over 18 percent of the total vote in the Security Council; and in 1966 this increased to three-fifteenths, or 20 percent. While not a majority, this is an important bloc of votes, certainly as compared to the earlier period.

Second, the African vote is often combined with the Asian vote against the colonial states. Whereas before 1966 the Asian group varied in strength between two and three votes, since 1965 it has always had three votes. When combined with the three African votes, this gives the Afro-Asian group six votes, or 40 percent of the total voting power, a not insignificant percentage.

Third, the influence of the Afro-Asian group in the Security Council is enhanced by the current three-way power struggle between the United States, the Soviet Union, and the People's Republic of China. Each power seeks the support of the uncommitted states, and each is willing to compromise on its short-range interests in order to enlarge its circle of friends. For this reason the three will support or at least not block the resolutions of the underdeveloped states on the North–South conflict.

Two factors assure the approval of Security Council condemnatory resolutions: a hard core of proponents and a larger group of states unwilling to antagonize them. The West has permitted the passage of resolutions condemning its members because it fears loss of influence with the uncommitted bloc. But one can readily see that the West has been relatively unenthusiastic about these resolutions from the fact that out of 45 condemnatory resolutions, members of the Western European/North American group abstained approximately 45 times, in comparison to the members of the Eastern European, Latin American, Asian, and African groups, whose abstention totals were four, six, one, and one, respectively.

Given the basic findings considered above, a fundamental question arises: Why have certain states been condemned when others that have committed similar actions were not? Why was

TABLE 3

Regional and Political Alignment in the Security Council, 1945-1974

Year of membership	Eastern European	Western European/ N. American	Latin American	Asian	African
Permanent	USSR	France United Kingdom United States		China*	
1946	Poland	Netherlands Australia†	Mexico Brazil		Egypt
1947	Poland	Australia† Belgium	Brazil Colombia	Syria‡	
1948	Ukraine	Belgium Canada	Colombia Argentina	Syria‡	
1949	Ukraine	Canada Norway	Argentina Cuba		Egypt‡
1950	Yugoslavia*	Norway	Cuba Ecuador	India	Egypt‡
1951	Yugoslavia*	Netherlands Turkey	Ecuador Brazil	India	Egypt‡
1952		Netherlands Turkey Greece	Brazil Chile	Pakistan	
1953		Greece Denmark	Chile Colombia	Pakistan Lebanon‡	
1954		Denmark Turkey New Zealand†	Colombia Brazil	Lebanon‡	

TABLE 3 (continued)

Year of membership	Eastern European	Western European/ N. American	Latin American	Asian	African
1955		Turkey New Zealand† Belgium	Brazil Peru	Iran	
1956	Yugoslavia	Belgium Australia†	Peru Cuba	Iran	
1957		Australia† Sweden	Cuba Colombia	Philippines Iraq‡	
1958		Sweden Canada	Colombia Panama	Iraq‡ Japan	
1959		Sweden Canada	Panama Argentina	Japan	Tunisia‡
1960	Poland	Italy	Argentina Italy	Ceylon	Tunisia‡
1961	Poland	Turkey	Ecuador Chile	Ceylon	Liberia UAR‡
1962	Romania	Ireland	Chile Venezuela		UAR‡ Ghana
1963		Norway	Venezuela Brazil	Philippines	Ghana Morocco‡
1964	Czechoslovakia	Norway	Brazil Bolivia		Morocco‡ Ivory Coast
1965		Netherlands	Bolivia Uruguay	Malaysia Jordan‡	Ivory Coast
1966	Bulgaria	Netherlands New Zealand†	Uruguay Argentina	Jordan‡ Japan	Mali Nigeria Uganda

Year					
1967	Bulgaria	Canada Denmark	Argentina Brazil	Japan India	Mali Nigeria Ethiopia
1968	Hungary	Canada Denmark	Brazil Paraguay	India Pakistan	Ethiopia Algeria Senegal
1969	Hungary	Finland Spain	Paraguay Colombia	Pakistan Nepal	Algeria Senegal Zambia
1970	Poland	Finland Spain	Colombia Nicaragua	Nepal Syria‡	Zambia Burundi Sierre Leone
1971	Poland	Belgium Italy	Argentina Nicaragua	Japan Syria‡	Burundi Sierre Leone Somalia
1972	Yugoslavia*	Belgium Italy	Argentina Panama	India† Japan	Guinea Somalia Sudan†
1973	Yugoslavia*	Australia† Austria	Panama Peru	India† Indonesia	Guinea Kenya Sudan†
1974	Byelorussian SSR	Australia† Austria	Costa Rica Peru	Indonesia Iraq‡	Kenya† Mauritania† Cameroon

*Nonaligned
†Politically tied with Commonwealth bloc
‡Politically tied with Arab bloc

West Pakistan not condemned for its massacres in East Pakistan; Nigeria for its repression of Biafra; the Sudan for its atrocities against its Negro population; Iraq for its oppression of its Kurdish population? Is morality in the United Nations no more than a relative standard tempered by the exigencies of the political situation? We return here to our original description of the United Nations as an institution that uniquely combines both the political and moral aspects of the international arena —with stress on the former where condemnatory resolutions are concerned. Every state that has been condemned has been in a negative political situation; that is, it has had a large group of states opposed to its existence or to its governing personnel and/or policies. But while a large group of enemy states is a necessary political factor, it is not sufficient for the approval of a condemnatory resolution. There must also be a moral factor: a policy or action that is judged to be morally wrong by most members of the world organization. *Both* factors are necessary for the passage of any condemnatory resolution; neither will suffice without the other, for the most part.

If we examine the cases of direct and indirect condemnations of the Soviet Union during the first decade and a half of UN history, we find that both the political and moral requirements for a condemnation were fulfilled. A large group of states— Western Europe—was bitterly opposed to the policies of the Soviet Union and fearful that the Soviet Union was a threat to its very survival. But it was the Soviet Union's restrictions on the flow of information that sparked a condemnatory resolution. Here, the political factor (fear and hatred of the Soviet Union) played a larger role than the moral factor (infringement of the freedom of information), which was not a grave offense in itself. The intensity of the fear made up for the weakness of the violation. By the time of the Hungarian Revolution, fear of the Soviet Union had somewhat diminished, thus weakening the political factor. However, in this case, the magnitude of the moral factor more than compensated for this.

Where the condemnations of South Africa are concerned there has been a convergence of political and moral factors. The African states are united against South Africa because of its policy of *apartheid* and its determination to retain South-West

Africa despite UN calls for its independence. Were there not a large African group in the United Nations, however, it is doubtful that South Africa would have been condemned for either reason. Its policy of *apartheid* was initiated in 1948, yet the United Nations waited until 1961 to condemn it. South Africa attempted to integrate South-West Africa in the late 1940s, was no more cooperative in the 1950s, yet was not condemned for its actions in regard to South-West Africa until 1962. Only since there has been a large bloc of African members antagonistic toward South Africa has the United Nations condemned the same actions that were at most deplored previously.

Portugal was first condemned in 1961, yet its policies toward its colonies have changed little in the last 500 years. One can cite two reasons for the change in world public opinion. First, other colonial states have altered their attitudes toward their colonies; Portugal has not, until recently. Second, the outbreak of guerrilla warfare in Angola in 1961 drew world attention to this area. Nevertheless, we must again consider the political factor: had there not been a large African membership in the United Nations it is doubtful that Portugal would ever have been condemned since, unlike all other states condemned within the last decade, it is an active member of the Western bloc. Because Portugal is not isolated in the United Nations, condemnations would seem unlikely; the fact that they have been approved attests to the strength of the African group.

Southern Rhodesia is a state with few friends and numerous foes, including the African group. Nevertheless, the moral factor involved in its condemnation was the unilateral declaration of independence by a small white minority in a state with a large black majority. The political factor was the opposition of a large group of African states. In the process of passing a series of UN condemnations, the United Kingdom was also condemned for not crushing the Southern Rhodesian government by force.

Finally, Israel has been repeatedly condemned. Like South Africa, it is isolated in the United Nations with few friends and powerful foes. This base of hostility and isolation has been a contributing factor to its condemnation. Yet despite this active hostility, there would have been few, if any, condemnations had Israel not carried out an active policy of reprisals. While these reprisals were not necessarily immoral in themselves, they, combined with the fact that Israel has numerous foes in the United Nations, provided the rationale for condemnations.

We should also analyze here the characteristics common to the states that have been condemned, at least as they have been perceived by their condemners.[8] They are generally considered the strongest in their respective areas, though perhaps not internationally. South Africa is the strongest state in Africa; Israel is militarily strongest in the Middle East; the Soviet Union is militarily overpowering; and the People's Republic of China is the dominant nation on the Southeast Asian continent.

Also, the state condemned has usually been relatively successful in quelling a revolution that the other states supported. It is often a prosperous state, certainly in comparison to its neighbors. The Soviet Union was successful in repressing the Hungarian Revolution; Portugal was successful, for a while, in repressing most revolutionary activity in Angola; Israel inflicted heavy casualties on the Fedayeen; and South Africa is the most prosperous state on the African continent.

In addition, the state condemned is considered threatening —precisely because it is successful and powerful. Thus the Arab states fear Israeli expansionism, and the African states are afraid that South Africa will attack the Northern black states.

There are several possible benefits, then, accruing to those states that condemn successful, powerful, and threatening neighbor states. A condemnation may relieve the frustration of failure felt by the leaders of the condemning states. It is a balm for the wounds inflicted by the enemy. The sense of failure can be somewhat alleviated and self-confidence restored by this demonstration of world moral support and sympathy.

A condemnatory resolution can be a useful domestic device for the government of a state because it creates a demonstrable victory. Despite the losses on the battlefield or the lags in development, the state has been victorious in the political field, in the United Nations. This victory can be explained to the people, thus overcoming some of the animosity directed toward the government for its failures.

Condemnatory resolutions may be used by a state to demonstrate that the enemy is morally wrong and that the whole outside world supports its cause. This may help to boost the morale of the armed forces as well as the population as a whole. Conversely, by having a foe condemned, states seek to lower the morale of the condemned state's population and its armed forces.

Condemnatory resolutions may lead to stronger resolutions. Many member states are increasingly frustrated by a state's consistent refusal to obey UN directives, especially if expressed in as strong a form as a condemnatory resolution. A climate is therefore created in which further steps such as expulsion, sanctions, or even the use of armed force may be proposed. These proposals are voiced with increasing urgency, making it progressively more difficult for the allies of the condemned state to block them. At some point in the future, then, the United Nations could take more stringent steps that would help the condemning states to defeat or humble their foes.

The condemning states may hope that a steady stream of condemnations will gradually create an international climate of opinion that will eventually legitimize an attack on the condemned state. Thus, repetition of condemnations may be intended to create a moral justification for war, as was the case with the Yom Kippur War in 1973.

Condemnatory resolutions may affect the policy of the condemned state, either in the short run or in the long run. Even minor changes are better than none at all; they may gradually lead to further minor concessions and, eventually, to major changes.

Finally, condemnatory resolutions are introduced because the sponsoring states can do little else. They are an act of desperation, an act taken because no other action is possible. Thus the United States pressed for the condemnation of the Soviet Union for its action in suppressing the 1956 Hungarian Revolution because it could do little else without incurring a serious risk of a new world war. The resolution was an expression of concern and support for the revolutionaries, yet it did not involve any risks. The same situation prevails in African condemnations of Portugal, South Africa, and Southern Rhodesia and in Arab condemnations of Israel. The condemnation is in many respects an admission of weakness and frustration.

In the case of pre-1960 condemnations, the West was by no means helpless against the East. It had a massive preponderance in nuclear arms, and it had other means outside the United Nations on which it could draw to defend its interests. The United States could utilize military and economic measures against the Soviet Union. America's troops fought in the Korean conflict; its military aid was sent to Greece and Turkey; its Marshall Plan helped Europe recover from the ravages of World War II, making it less susceptible to communism. Much of the struggle against the East thus took place outside the United Nations. Only when the United States felt most helpless against the Soviet bloc did it resort to condemnatory resolutions—that is, during the Communist Chinese drive into South Korea and the Soviet invasion of Hungary.

The African states, on the other hand, have no recourse other than the United Nations in their effort to eliminate colonialism. They do not possess the military means to force the colonial states to alter their policies. So they turn to the United Nations for two reasons: in the hope that they can influence the allies of the colonial states to press for changes in their policies, and for lack of any alternative. The resort to UN condemnations is a measure of their desperation and helplessness. The Security Council condemnations of Israel are also evidence that some states can do nothing else; the number of these condemnations has risen sharply since the 1967 war (five from 1948 to 1967, eight from 1968 to 1970). The Arab states cannot prevent Israel from incorporating the old city of Jerusalem into the new one, so they condemn Israel for it. They cannot prevent Israel's reprisals, so again, they resort to condemnations.

A related explanation for the increase in condemnatory resolutions should also be examined. The Western states did not place a great degree of confidence in the United Nations after their disastrous experience with its predecessor, the League of Nations. Since they had created the United Nations, they were cognizant of its shortcomings. The African states, on the other hand, were created in the age of the United Nations and, to a great degree, *by* the United Nations. They place great confidence in this organization; having had no previous experience with international organizations, they look upon the United Nations as the great hope of mankind.[9] In a sense the Western states have had little confidence in the United Nations precisely because they created it, while the Southern states have had great confidence in the United Nations because it created many of them.

In the first fifteen years of the United Nation's existence, the United States, despite its reservations, demonstrated the use of condemnations, using the United Nations to condemn the Soviet bloc. Gradually the leaders of the new states, then students in the United States or in other Western states, became infected with a faith in the United Nations, which is reflected in their later policies toward that organization. The manifold condemnations of the last decade and a half may therefore be due to earlier American inspiration.

2

Case Studies

It would be helpful at this point to examine some specific condemnatory resolutions. Research for this book covered resolutions condemning six states—the People's Republic of China, the Soviet Union, Portugal, Rhodesia, the Republic of South Africa, and Israel; however, considerations of space make an exhaustive discussion of all these cases impossible. I have chosen to discuss three: one pre-1960 Security Council resolution—resolution 498 (1951), condemning the Communist Chinese drive into South Korea; an early post-1960 General Assembly resolution—resolution 1805 (1962), condemning South Africa for its internal policy of *apartheid* and its refusal to grant South-West Africa independence; and a more recent resolution, typical of many that have been issued against Israel in the ongoing Mideast situation—Security Council resolution 256 (1968), condemning an Israeli retaliatory raid.

The People's Republic of China has been condemned three times by the United Nations, all during the period 1951 through 1954, in relation to its actions in Korea: on February 1, 1951, in resolution 498, for its intervention in the Korean conflict; on December 3, 1953, in resolution 804 (following a series of reports of Communist Chinese atrocities against UN prisoners of war captured in Korea) for the alleged mistreatment and torture (by North Korea and the People's Republic of China) of these prisoners; and on December 10, 1954, in resolution 906, for the detention and trial of eleven United States airmen associated with the UN command in Korea.

Resolution 498 was a crisis condemnation passed in response to the sudden Communist Chinese attack on UN forces in North Korea, November 1950. Neither the word "condemn" nor "censure" appeared in its text; instead this resolution found the People's Republic of China guilty of aggression—one of the gravest charges that can be leveled against a state. As indicated earlier, a resolution of condemnation generally consists of two parts, a judgment of guilt and an actual rebuke; in the accusation of aggression the mere announcement is so severe as to be a rebuke in itself. Thus resolution 498 is considered a condemnation. An analysis of General Assembly resolution 498, then, will provide a good illustration of the way in which a crisis condemnatory resolution evolves; in addition, the passage of time has given us some perspective on the objectives, stated and tacit, of the various UN members involved in the situation, and whether or not the resolution bore them out.

The Republic of South Africa has been condemned more often, directly and indirectly, than any other state in the United Nations—22 times directly and many more times indirectly, in conjunction with other colonial states in the period 1961 through 1970. Two ongoing situations have precipitated these condemnations: South Africa's domestic *apartheid* policy, and its refusal to grant independence to South-West Africa; in addition, its application of *apartheid* to South-West Africa has aroused a great deal of opposition. With the outbreak of guerrilla warfare in Angola and South Rhodesia's unilateral declaration of independence, attention has tended to focus on Southern Africa and the number and variety of condemnations has increased.

Despite the many condemnations that have been issued against South Africa during this period, I intend to consider only resolution 1805 (1962)—first, because the motivations precipitating its proposal and the debate preceding its passage are similar to those that attended the condemnations that came after it; and second, because its position in the series of condemnations that involve essentially the same issues points up the self-perpetuating nature of the condemnatory process itself. In contrast to resolution 498, which was a crisis condemnation, the direct result of the Communist Chinese intervention in North Korea against UN forces, resolution 1805 was a situation condemnation, not inspired by any one specific action. It was the result of a general long-range policy in South Africa, and continuing General Assembly admonitions to South Africa

to alter that policy. Resolution 498 was approved in response
to a crisis taking place outside the United Nations. Resolution
1805 was a condemnation for failure to heed UN suggestions,
and the action took place, to a large extent, within the confines
of the United Nations. Analysis of this situation can give us
some idea of what effects a long series of condemnations can
actually have on the states involved, for good or ill.

Security Council resolution 256 (1968), condemning Israel
for its policy of retaliation against Jordan, was one of many
such resolutions issued against that state. Examination of the
situation, as represented by this particular resolution, gives us
an idea of what serious damage ineffectual condemnatory resolutions can do to the United Nations itself in terms of prestige
and successful future interventions.

THE PEOPLE'S REPUBLIC OF CHINA
Resolution 498 (1951)

In 1945 Korea was occupied by American and Soviet troops.
The Americans had accepted the surrender of Japanese troops
south of the 38th parallel and the Russians did the same north
of that parallel. The two powers then agreed to set up a joint
commission to establish a government, but the commission was
quickly deadlocked. On November 14, 1947, the General Assembly created a nine-member temporary commission to facilitate both the establishment of a unified government in Korea
by means of elections and the withdrawal of all foreign troops
from that state. However, members of the Soviet bloc refused
to cooperate in the endeavor. The commission observed elections in South Korea and these eventually led to the formation
of a government on August 15, 1948. But the commission was
refused permission to enter North Korea, which set up its own
government in September.

In December the General Assembly declared that the South
Korean government was the only legitimate government in Korea. It again recommended the withdrawal of all foreign troops

from Korea and established a seven-man commission for the unification of Korea.

By July 1949 the UN Commission on Korea reported that it had not been able to make any progress toward unification. It had observed the withdrawal of the United States forces, but the Soviet Union insisted that the General Assembly had no right to act on the Korean question: since Korea was discussed in the Moscow Agreement it should be dealt with by the Allied Commission. The UN Commission on Korea was illegal and would not be allowed to enter North Korea.

In October 1949 the UN Commission on Korea was assigned the task of observing and reporting any developments that might lead to a military conflict in the area.

On June 25, 1950 North Korean forces invaded South Korea. The Security Council called an emergency session and determined that the attack was a breach of the peace. By a vote of nine in favor, with Yugoslavia opposed and the Soviet Union absent, it called for an immediate cease-fire and the withdrawal of all North Korean forces. It also requested that UN members assist in implementing the resolution. Two days later the Security Council adopted an American-sponsored resolution by 7 to 0, with Yugoslavia abstaining and the Soviet Union absent, recommending that UN members give all assistance to South Korea so as to enable it to repel the armed attack. The United States ordered its air and sea forces to support the South Korean forces and finally ordered a naval blockade and the use of ground forces.

Fifty-one states supported the Security Council; five declared the June 27th resolution illegal because of the absence of two permanent members of the Security Council. Nevertheless, on July 7, by a vote of 7 to 0, with Egypt, India, and Yugoslavia abstaining and the Soviet Union absent, the Security Council requested all states providing military forces to place them under a United States unified command.

Despite troop contributions by sixteen states, the UN forces steadily retreated into an ever-diminishing area of the Korean peninsula until an amphibious landing at Inchon broke the deadly vise and enabled the UN troops to begin a rapid advance.

As UN forces neared the 38th parallel the United States decided to have them advance into and occupy North Korea, thereby unifying the entire peninsula. Toward this end the General Assembly established the UN Commission for the Unification and Rehabilitation of Korea (the Security Council having been deadlocked since August 1 by the return of the Soviet representative). This commission was to establish a unified, independent, democratic Korea, and the goal was clearly in sight as the UN forces drove ever deeper into North Korea.

On November 6, 1950, the Security Council was notified through a special report of the Unified Command that there were Communist Chinese forces among the North Korean troops. The United Nations had given assurances to the government of the People's Republic of China that its border would be considered inviolate. Nevertheless, Communist Chinese forces moved in and shortly thereafter launched a full-scale attack on the UN forces, driving them back and toward South Korea.

On December 14 the General Assembly passed resolution 384 in the hope that it would halt the conflict in Korea. It created a Group on Cease-Fire in Korea that attempted to establish contact with General Wu, the Communist Chinese representative to the United Nations. On December 21 the People's Republic of China refused this request, charging that the Group on Cease-Fire in Korea had been illegally constituted owing to the absence of Communist China from the United Nations. The Group on Cease-Fire in Korea had meanwhile addressed another message to Foreign Minister Chou En-lai on December 19 offering to begin negotiations on the pacific settlement of all Far Eastern questions as soon as hostilities were terminated. Chou En-lai replied on December 22 that the Group on Cease-Fire in Korea was illegal, and he set certain indispensable conditions for settlement of the Korean problem, including the withdrawal of foreign troops from Taiwan and the admission of the People's Republic of China to the United Nations.

While charges were being answered with countercharges the UN troops were retreating in the face of Communist Chinese attacks. By December 26, 1950 the Communist Chinese troops had reached and crossed the 38th parallel. On January 1, 1951 a Communist Chinese offensive was launched, driving the UN forces from Seoul back across the Han River. By January 25, 1951 the line had stabilized and a general UN counter-offensive began which was not to be stopped until the UN forces reached the 38th parallel in March.

On January 13, the First Committee had approved a supplementary report of the Group on Cease-Fire in Korea and sent it to the People's Republic of China. This report consisted of a statement of principles for the establishment of a cease-fire. It called for the withdrawal of foreign troops from Korea, in accordance with UN principles, to permit the carrying out of General Assembly resolution 376 (V) "that Korea should be a unified, independent, democratic, sovereign State with a Constitution and a government based on free popular elections." And finally, it provided for the creation of an "appropriate body," including "representatives of the Governments of the United Kingdom, the United States of America, the Union of Soviet Socialist Republics, and the People's Republic of China" for the settlement of Far Eastern questions, among them "the representation of China at the United Nations." [1]

Foreign Minister Chou En-lai replied on January 17, 1951, proposing to the United Nations that negotiations "be held among the countries concerned on the basis of agreement to the withdrawal of all foreign troops from Korea and the settlement of Korean domestic affairs by the Korean people themselves in order to put an end to the hostilities in Korea at an early date." He also proposed that these negotiations "include the withdrawal of United States armed forces from Taiwan and the Taiwan Straits and Far Eastern related problems"; that the countries participating in these negotiations be "the People's Republic of China, the Soviet Union, the United Kingdom, the United States of America, France, India, and Egypt . . . [with] the rightful place of the Central People's Government of the People's Republic of China in the United Nations . . . established as from the beginning of the seven-nation conference"; and finally, that "the seven-nation conference be held in China." [2]

Shortly after the First Committee began consideration of the Communist Chinese reply, two draft resolutions were introduced in the General Assembly: the representative of the United States proposed a resolution in which the General Assembly would condemn the People's Republic of China for aggression in Korea, while Afghanistan, Burma, Egypt, India, Indonesia, Iran, Iraq, Lebanon, Pakistan, Saudi Arabia, Syria, and Yemen introduced a resolution proposing that representatives of Egypt, France, the People's Republic of China, the Soviet Union, the United Kingdom, and the United States meet as soon as possible to clarify and amplify the Communist Chinese reply and to make arrangements for a peaceful settlement.

Lebanon proposed two amendments to the American resolution—the first to change the wording from "rejected all" UN proposals to has "not accepted" UN proposals, thus implying that the Communist Chinese reply was not a total rejection; the second to add a paragraph clearly stating that if the Good Offices Committee reported satisfactory progress the Ad Hoc Committee on Collective Measures would be authorized to defer its report. The United States accepted the Lebanese amendments, thus modifying the resolution.

The Soviet Union submitted several amendments to the twelve-power resolution, proposing to delete the heading "Intervention of the People's Republic of China in Korea," and to specify that any meeting of the seven powers could be called only by the President of the General Assembly in agreement with the participants. A further revision stated that the seven powers should agree upon a cease-fire arrangement at the first meeting, deferring other matters until this was done. The Soviet Union further proposed that after agreement on the cease-fire had been reached, the meeting should proceed to arranging the withdrawal of all foreign forces from Korea so that the Korean people could settle their own affairs; the withdrawal of American forces from Taiwan; and to discussing general questions relating to the Far East. The twelve-power resolution eventually failed to be adopted; the American resolution, with the Lebanese amendments, was approved by a vote of 44 to 7 with eight abstentions.

In the general debate on these resolutions and their amendments the Western states generally supported the United States resolution, the Asian states pressed for the adoption of the twelve-power resolution, and the Soviet bloc opposed both. The controversy raged around three issues: establishing the guilt of one party, examining the effect of the draft resolution on the future situation, and analyzing the effect of the draft resolution on the United Nations itself.

Most Western states stressed the fact that the People's Republic of China was the aggressor. It had deliberately and willfully attacked UN forces without provocation, had violated the UN Charter, and was openly defying the United Nations. The Asian states argued that the case was not so clear-cut. There was much evidence that the People's Republic of China had attacked UN troops not from a desire for aggression but from a pervasive fear of the UN forces which were steadily approaching its border. True, no one could excuse the North Korean action, which was clearly aggressive, but the Communist Chinese case had some justification. Its action was a form of self-defense and could not truly be considered aggression.

The Soviet bloc denied that the People's Republic of China was in any conceivable way the aggressor. The United States was clearly the aggressor because it was using the United Nations as its tool. The United States wanted war and utilized the Korean episode as an excuse. The Communist Chinese proposals were constructive but the United States had immediately rejected them, even though there had been little time for deliberation. The United States was afraid of peace.

The reason for the intense controversy on this point is obvious. Since condemnation is essentially a judgment of wrongdoing and a rebuke for it, and since a judgment is the attribution of guilt to one party, this stage of the debate was critical to all sides.

After establishing the guilt of one of the parties, the next step in the condemnatory process is the pronouncement of a rebuke to the guilty party. Before taking such a step, however, the United Nations, as a responsible international actor, must always assess the effects of such a step. The essential purpose of the United Nations is to promote international peace, not to condemn; therefore the members must carefully weigh the consequences of the latter act. Since the American draft resolution actually condemned the People's Republic of China for aggression, an assessment of its possible effects on future negotiations caused more problems than the discussion of the other resolutions proposed.

The Western states insisted that the United States resolution would not prevent negotiations in the future. The United Nations was merely stating the facts of the case in this resolution; in fact, its latter paragraphs actually encouraged negotiations. After all, the Western states added, the People's Republic of China had often condemned the United Nations for aggression in Korea yet the United Nations remained willing to negotiate.

The Asian states claimed that the United States draft resolution would eliminate any purpose for future negotiations since the United Nations would have unilaterally determined the guilt of its opponent before negotiations had even begun. Besides, how could the United Nations label a state an aggressor yet willingly negotiate with it? Such post-condemnation negotiations would degrade the United Nations in the eyes of the world, and the organization would stand accused of appeasement. A more moderate resolution (such as the twelve-power draft resolution) would leave the United Nations more room for maneuvering since a peaceful settlement of the dispute would remain a possibility.

The Soviet bloc insisted that the United States resolution would end all hope of negotiations. Therefore, the United Nations was faced with a choice: It could condemn the People's Republic of China (unjustly, of course) and thus eliminate any chances for negotiations, or it could decide to negotiate.

An additional factor considered in the debate was the effect of any resolution on the United Nations itself. It would be imprudent to approve a resolution that might negatively affect the authority and prestige of the United Nations. For example, a resolution might itself be defective because the particular UN organ that approved it did not have the authority to do so or because the United Nations received a misleading assessment of the facts and therefore reached an erroneous conclusion. Or the United Nations might reach the correct conclusion and make valid recommendations, but be incapable of implementing the resolution, thus allowing the state concerned to disregard the resolution. This would raise doubts as to the efficacy and validity of all UN resolutions and diminish their value in future situations.

The Western states insisted that it was essential for the future viability of the United Nations to condemn the People's Republic of China as an aggressor. Failure to do so would be appeasement, an act that could very well sound the death knell of the United Nations, just as it had the League of Nations. Furthermore, concessions to such aggression might hasten the advent of World War III.

The Asian states contended that a condemnation for aggression would accomplish little, merely decreasing UN prestige. The fact that the People's Republic of China finally seemed to be amenable to negotiation precluded any condemnation, which would be incompatible with the raison d'être of the organization—peace through negotiations. If the People's Republic of China were to be condemned yet continue to oppose the UN forces, the organization would be exposed as ineffective, and the image of impotence so created would decrease its authority and prestige. The Asian states therefore supported the twelve-power resolution urging negotiations.

The Soviet bloc contended that the American draft resolution would be not only useless but also illegal under the UN Charter since the General Assembly had no authority to determine the aggressor and therefore no power to condemn it. According to Article 39 of the Charter, only the Security Council can determine that an act of aggression has actually taken place. The resolution was invalid since the United Nations was merely acting as a branch of the United States Department of State. American policy was attempting to transform the United Nations into its instrument and thus effectively destroy that organization. The fact that the United Nations was already slavishly following American policy cast doubts upon its international character, thus damaging its authority and prestige.

A condemnatory resolution, then, is disputed first in terms of what actually happened. When the guilt of one party has been established, the dispute centers on what procedure to take. The first arguments attempt to facilitate or impede the judgment of guilt by variously interpreting the substantive facts of the case; the second concentrate on promoting or preventing a rebuke. In this case the procedural argument was whether to condemn the People's Republic of China or to settle the matter by other methods, inside or outside the United Nations.

There was a general alignment in the debate with respect to all three resolutions issued against the People's Republic of China: the Western European and American states pressed for a condemnation, the Soviet bloc attempted to prevent the passage of such a resolution, and the Asian states urged moderation. On resolution 498, fourteen of the fifteen Western European states voted for the resolution. Sweden, consistent with its policy of neutrality, abstained from voting. All twenty members of the Latin American group voted in favor of the resolution. Five out of the six Eastern European members voted against the resolution. Yugoslavia abstained, indicating its estrangement from the Soviet bloc.

Of the fourteen Asian members, seven voted for the resolution: China (Taiwan), Iran, Iraq, Israel, Lebanon, the Philippines, and Thailand, all states leaning toward the West, if not actually in that camp.[3] Two Asian states, India and Burma, voted against the resolution, and five abstained—Afghanistan, Indonesia, Pakistan, Syria, and Yemen. Of these, only Pakistan can be said to have been aligned with the West; the rest were either neutral or pro-East. One Asian state, Saudi Arabia, was absent. Of the four African states, three voted with the West. Of these three, the Union of South Africa is closely aligned with the West and both Ethiopia and Liberia are generally pro-Western. Egypt, the only abstaining African member, was in a neutralist position.

Thus in the voting as well as in the debate the Western and pro-Western states supported the American draft resolution condemning the People's Republic of China, the Soviet bloc opposed it, and the neutralist states took a position between the two groups.

The resolution condemning the People's Republic of China was strongly supported by the United States although many of its allies were less than enthusiastic about the entire procedure and there was no significant groundswell of support. Although the United States had already pressed for a condemnation in early January its allies insisted on making one last attempt to gain a cease-fire. It was only after this bid was rejected by the People's Republic of China on January 17 that they agreed reluctantly to go along with the American-sponsored resolution.

The members' aversion to needlessly antagonizing the People's Republic of China is understandable; they did not want to increase the scope of the conflict. But what were the aims of the United States? What did it hope to accomplish by this resolution?

In analyzing the grounds for a condemnatory resolution one must distinguish between the official reasons, repeated endlessly in the debate, and other reasons which, although not stated explicitly, are no less important and often more so. No state is willing to admit that the resolution it sponsors would benefit its own narrow national interests. Yet the fact remains that states would rarely devote time and effort to proposing and lobbying for a resolution if there were not some national incentive for it. On the other hand, few states will vote for a resolution merely because another state will benefit from it. Therefore, in an effort to win support, states will often try to cloak the true reasons for their resolutions in the mantle of the general good.

Since it is in the United Nations that these resolutions are passed, the general good is often defined as the good of the organization.[4] Sponsors and supporters will attempt to prove that their resolution reflects the will of the Charter and/or will enhance the authority and prestige of the United Nations. Conversely, they say, failure to pass their resolution will violate the principles of the organization and/or decrease its authority and prestige.[5] Thus the United States often proclaimed that resolution 498 was in accord with the principles of the United Nations, an institution designed to deter aggression through the unified action of its member states against the aggressor.

> No nation was strong enough to stand alone and unaided: the weak depended on the strong and the strong depended on the weak. Security was indivisible. The United Nations could not let one nation fall a victim to aggression and at the same time believe that it would be possible to protect another nation on the next occasion. If the organization

acted in that way, the very principle of collective security would be destroyed. The peoples of the world would not only turn away from the United Nations but would lose faith in the interdependence of nations. . . . One of the fundamental principles of the Charter was the outlawing of aggression and it was therefore right that the United Nations should, by its determination, decisions and actions prove that no power could defy that principle with impunity. The whole world expected the United Nations to conform to that principle. The time for action had come, as any further delay might permanently destroy the unity of the organization.

After a long and careful study of the problems involved the United States Government considered that the United Nations should not evade its duty to face the aggression committed by the Chinese communists.[6]

In many ways this was indeed a basic reason for United States pressure to condemn the People's Republic of China. Many members of the United States government, especially Ambassador Austin, were truly dedicated to UN principles. It was their faith in the organization, in its moral righteousness, that convinced many officials that the United Nations must indeed condemn the People's Republic of China.[7] "I was convinced," said President Truman, "that to have ignored the appeal of Korea for aid, to have stood aside from the assault upon the Charter, would have meant the end of the United Nations as a shield against aggression. It might have meant the end of any possibility that collective security could be made to work."[8]

The United States argued that the purpose of resolution 498 was to *recognize* aggression. If aggression were not recognized, the entire concept of collective security could not be initiated, thus destroying the very foundations of the United Nations. By demonstrating that collective security could be implemented, a declaration of aggression was a viable method of preventing or terminating aggression. Resolution 498 would enhance the authority and prestige of the United Nations, thus benefiting all states concerned.[9]

These were the official arguments. There were also several other basic reasons for United States support of the resolutions condemning the People's Republic of China.

Internationally, the United States saw several clear benefits deriving from a resolution condemning the People's Republic of China. For one thing, it would demonstrate to the world the seriousness of the Communist menace. The United Nations was an avowedly impartial body in the East–West conflict; if that organization were to publicly proclaim that the Communist states were guilty of aggression, the United States would not only gain a diplomatic victory, but the condemnation might serve as a deterrent to future aggression if the diplomatic loss to the People's Republic of China outweighed any military gain.[10] This objective was a fairly important one to American leaders at a time when the fear of Communist expansionism was paramount.

A UN declaration of Communist aggression might also garner additional support for the UN forces by theretofore inactive states, and perhaps alert the Asian states to the dangers of further Communist expansion, thus inducing them to become more active in support of UN efforts in South Korea.[11]

Another advantage of a condemnatory resolution was that it would encourage states, of whatever size, to resist Communist encroachments by demonstrating that the free world was ready to support such resistance against any aggressor, large or small. Indeed, the argument was often used in the First Committee debate that the United Nations had accused North Korea, a small state, of aggression so it must now recognize aggression by a large state, the People's Republic of China.

The resolution would also demonstrate to the Communist world the determination of the free world in Korea.[12] After all, the Communist states could not fail to notice that a resolution advocating a more moderate approach on the Korean question was defeated by this far stronger resolution. The United States could hardly be expected to sponsor this resolution and then engage in a precipitate withdrawal. It was thus a signal that the Western states intended to remain in Korea even under the most adverse circumstances, a public declaration of American policy that might well encourage the People's Republic of China and the Soviet Union to adjust their policies accordingly.

An additional advantage of such a resolution was that it

would be justification for war if the United States should decide to declare war in Korea. Thus President Truman, in a news conference on January 4, 1951, declared that the United States would not attack the People's Republic of China without UN authority as well as a formal declaration of war by Congress.

Such a resolution might also deflate Communist Chinese prestige, which had been greatly enhanced by victories around the world; the United Nations would go on record as saying that the policy of the People's Republic of China, even if successful in this instance, was morally wrong, thus depriving the state of the political and propaganda advantages of victory. Further, coupled with an economic embargo, such a resolution might interfere with extended military operations as well as with the ambitious program of industrial expansion envisaged by the Communist Chinese leaders since it would make more difficult the importation of materials essential for the creation of a modern industrial state.[13]

A condemnation might also serve as a symbol of support and a morale booster for the UN troops in Korea.[14] And the possibility existed that the People's Republic of China would actually moderate its policy in response to the strong international moral and diplomatic pressure exerted by a UN condemnation and perhaps halt its offensives.[15]

Domestically, resolution 498 would legitimize the urgent and rapid build-up of the armed forces both to other states and to the American population itself. Such international support of the United States' contention that the People's Republic of China was indeed the aggressor would serve as a further vindication of the military build-up and state of national emergency that then existed, substantiating the American people's fear of the Communist menace and therefore diminishing domestic opposition.[16]

An additional benefit would be to diminish public pressure for stronger action in the Korean conflict. Senate resolution 35, passed on January 23, 1951, stated that "it is the sense of the Senate that the United Nations should immediately declare Communist China an aggressor in Korea." The House of Representatives had passed a similar resolution four days earlier. The *New York Times,* a notably liberal newspaper, demanded that the People's Republic of China be branded an aggressor by the United Nations and criticized that organization for not having done so.[17]

At the time of the actual passage of this resolution, February 1, 1951, the UN forces were already on the offensive; but when the resolution was formulated a month earlier, these forces were being driven back and suffering heavy losses. Thus the original intent was political victory when military victory seemed out of reach, to enhance the image of the United Nations in the eyes of the American public, and to raise the morale of the American people themselves. The steady stream of defeats had inspired a certain pessimism in the United States. Questions were being raised as to the utility of the United Nations in a bipolar world and the entire concept of an impartial international organization had come under severe and critical scrutiny.

Finally, there were several advantages to be had from this condemnation within the UN arena itself. The most direct was that it would prepare the way for future, stronger resolutions. It would also serve as a reaffirmation of previous UN resolutions. Throughout this period, every United States action was backed by a UN resolution. The use of armed force to defend South Korea was recommended by Security Council resolutions 83 and 84, and the entry of the UN forces into North Korea was sanctioned by General Assembly resolution 376. An additional, stronger condemnation would buttress previous resolutions and reaffirm the legality of the presence of UN forces in Korea. Thus this resolution would be part of the UN diplomatic umbrella being created to justify Western actions to counter Soviet aggressiveness.

Resolution 498 would serve to deny the People's Republic of China a seat in the United Nations.[18] There was much disagreement between the United States and the United Kingdom on this point. The United Kingdom believed that the presence of Communist Chinese representatives in the United Nations at this time might be very useful. The United States' position was that granting membership would be tantamount to rewarding the Communist Chinese for aggression. Since the UN Charter specifically states that "Membership in the United Nations is open to all other peace-loving states which accept the obligations contained in the present Charter and, in the judgment of the organization, are able and willing to carry out these obligations," [19] a resolution condemning the People's Republic of China for aggression would greatly reduce that state's chances for UN membership.[20]

Another benefit of such a resolution would be the effective rebuttal of all Communist Chinese claims of American aggression, and all Communist arguments for a UN condemnation of the United States.[21] Obviously, the event of such a condemnation was unlikely, but the charges were annoying and resolution 498 would openly demonstrate their hypocrisy.

One must also take into account the momentum of the situation in the United Nations, which exerted its own pressure on the United States with respect to this resolution. The United Nations had repeatedly called for a cease-fire, and each request had been ignored by the People's Republic of China. In light of these previous resolutions, the United Nations was forced to move further, the logical next step being a condemnation for aggression.[22]

In considering the various reasons for the American sponsorship of resolution 498, it is apparent that one resolution could not satisfy all United States' objectives. But resolution 498 could contribute to the fulfillment of these goals, if only marginally in some areas. The resolution was part of the international political campaign being waged at the time, a campaign perhaps as important to the outcome of the war as the military campaign.

Nevertheless, a resolution's effectiveness must be measured ultimately in terms of the original objectives of its supporters. Resolution 498 ordered the People's Republic of China to withdraw its forces from Korea; called upon all states to lend every assistance to the UN action and to refrain from giving any assistance to the aggressor in Korea; and requested that the members of the Collective Measures Committee consider additional measures to defeat the aggressor and report back to the General Assembly.

Interestingly enough, the states engaged in hostilities against the United Nations ignored the relevant parts of the resolution.

The People's Republic of China had not seen fit to heed moderate resolutions; why should it comply with a condemnation? As a matter of fact, on February 2, 1951 Foreign Minister Chou En-lai charged that General Assembly resolution 498 blocked the only chances of a peaceful settlement and was in any case invalid since Communist China had not participated in the debate. He said his country would pay no heed to the Good Offices Committee. He further declared that the United States coerced the United Nations into passing resolution 498 and had engineered the entire Korean conflict by invading and intervening in Korea and Formosa.[23]

On February 16, 1951, in an article in *Pravda,* the Soviet party newspaper, Premier Stalin denounced the United Nations for branding the People's Republic of China as an aggressor. He said that the United Nations could not threaten the People's Republic of China with armed force since it was already being used against that state. Thus there was no plausible threat available that would deter the People's Republic of China from continuing its actions. Moreover, the Soviet Union could hardly be expected to stop its aid because of the UN resolution.[24]

On the other hand, while most of the states supporting the UN action in Korea reacted favorably to resolution 498 and were cooperative in implementing its requests, the Western states would probably have continued to support the UN without the resolution. In fact, many of these states were opposed to the resolution and supported it only because of American pressure. Denmark and Australia were unenthusiastic; the United Kingdom and France were unwilling to act as co-sponsors; and Canada and Israel backed amendments that would have severely diluted the resolution. Indeed, the *New York Times* on January 24 reported that several Western states actually backed the twelve-nation resolution against the United States resolution. According to Secretary Acheson,

> We supported this plan in the fervent hope and belief that the Chinese would reject it (as they did) and that our allies would then return (as they did) to comparative sanity and follow us in censuring the Chinese as aggressors. . . . At once the political roof fell in, and . . . Senator

Taft attacked us with great violence. . . . The resolution
proposed on January 11 and adopted on the thirteenth was
rejected four days later by the Chinese. Our allies—rather
grudgingly as they believed that the United States was get-
ting the best of both worlds when the State Department
supported the five principles and the country rejected
them—joined us on February 1 in passing a condemnation
of Chinese aggression but dragged their feet until May in
taking any action to punish the aggressor.[25]

Significantly, no state began to assist the UN forces just because
of this resolution.

Although there was no overt reaction by the states neutral in
the Korean conflict, of three members of this group appointed to
the Additional Measures Committee, Burma and Yugoslavia
refused to serve. Thus the committee consisted of twelve members: seven from Western Europe, three from Latin America,
one from Africa, and one from Asia—all, with the exception of
Egypt, solidly in the Western camp. India and Canada, the two
states named to the Good Offices Committee, formally declined
to serve on that committee.

With respect to the international effects of this resolution,
armistice talks did begin in the same year that resolution 498
was passed. However, this was not due so much to the resolution's request for a Communist Chinese withdrawal from Korea
than to the recognition by both sides that no significant advance
would be made against the other. It was probably the failure
of Communist China's fifth phase offensive at the end of May
1951 that convinced it to agree to cease-fire negotiations in
June since these negotiations had been dragging on for two
years after the passage of a condemnatory resolution and one
advocating sanctions.

The resolution also publicized the fact that the Communists
were guilty of aggression, and in this way it was a political
victory for the United States. It is difficult to assert, however,
that the unfavorable publicity actually deterred future Communist aggressions. More likely, it was the combination of successful military resistance to the Communist Chinese actions in
Korea and the deterrent effect of nuclear weapons.

The resolution had some success in deflating Communist
Chinese prestige. A public condemnation of a state was taken

very seriously at the time, as evidenced by the long and bitter debate over this resolution. Nevertheless, the military events in the Korean peninsula affected Communist Chinese prestige far more than did any UN resolution.

Resolution 498 did not win any allies for the United States in the Korean conflict. The Asian states vigorously opposed the American resolution, twelve of them sponsoring a far more moderate resolution. Prime Minister Nehru of India denounced the resolution time and again during this period. Many states feared that resolutions such as this one would prevent compromise and inexorably lead to a third world war.

Despite the defeat of the Asian resolution, the fact that two out of three neutral states refused to serve on the Additional Measures Committee is indicative of their lack of enthusiasm for the war effort.

The resolution also had little effect on Communist China's relations with the Soviet Union. A Treaty of Friendship, Alliance and Mutual Assistance had been signed by the two nations in February 1950 and ratified in September of the same year. In addition, the Soviet Union sent more than $2 billion in military aid [26] and transferred various properties in Peking, Kairen, and the Northeast to the People's Republic of China free of charge. Further, trade between the two nations doubled from 1950 to 1951.[27] After Stalin's death in 1953 Soviet aid increased even further.

Thus there was an increasingly close relationship between the People's Republic of China and the Soviet Union at least until 1956. The Communist Chinese intervention in Korea certainly did not weaken this alliance and in all probability strengthened it, particularly if one accepts the assumption that the Soviet Union masterminded the Korean conflict. Moreover, if this assumption is valid, resolution 498 indirectly condemned the Soviet Union, because extending aid to the aggressors was in fact committing aggression indirectly.[28]

Finally, although the resolution was intended to improve the morale of the UN forces in Korea, and there was indeed a sharp upturn in morale in February, it is difficult to credit resolution 498 for this. The morale boost was due rather to General Ridgway's leadership and the victories on the battlefield. While the resolution might have been used as justification for a formal declaration of war, the United States government decided that it would be wiser not to do so. Moreover, later events showed there was no need to declare war.

On the domestic front, resolution 498 did provide the administration one justification, among others, for the urgent and rapid build-up of the American military machine. After all, the United Nations itself had recognized the Communist menace; the United States had to take drastic measures for its own protection. It is important to note, however, that although this resolution served to justify American actions, these actions were determined by events on the Korean peninsula. Both the state of national emergency and the rearmament program had begun long before resolution 498.

The resolution did not put an end to the demand for UN action; however, it satisfied many critics and protected the United Nations from further extremist demands to dissolve it. Still, one cannot discount the success of the Eighth Army in Korea at this time, which was probably at least as important as resolution 498 in diminishing demands for drastic action. Continued defeats would have made the demands more vociferous and more widespread.

Finally, although resolution 498 provided an undeniable morale boost on the home front, battlefield victories contributed far more. The resolution was one small factor that captured the headlines for a few days and was quickly forgotten. News from the battlefront, on the other hand, was constantly displayed by all the mass media, and it was the most important factor in improving domestic morale.

The argument most often used in favor of this resolution is that it upheld the UN Charter. But consider: while the United Nations was meant to deter or halt aggression, the very existence of the veto implies that it was not meant to mediate great-power conflicts. Thus, although technically in congruence with the Charter, this resolution actually violated its essence by transforming the United Nations into an instrument of the East-West conflict.

Another objective of this condemnatory resolution was to increase the prestige of the United Nations, and it is true that by denouncing aggression wherever it existed the United Nations gained stature in the eyes of the world. However, it was not denunciation but military victories that stopped the Communist Chinese forces and enhanced UN prestige. A mere condemnation of aggression followed by abandonment of South Korea or by a military defeat of UN forces would have been a disaster. In fact, the entire Korean episode may have resulted in a net decrease in UN prestige if it became apparent to most people that the United Nations could not effectively cope with great-power aggression.[29]

On the other hand, resolution 498 did reinforce earlier resolutions asking states to aid South Korea, and in this way, it was a further legitimization of United States action. In fact, the resolution not only justified Western actions against aggression, but also laid the foundation for resolution 500, approved on May 18, 1951:

The General Assembly
1. Recommends that every state:
(a) Apply an embargo on the shipment to areas under the control of the Central People's Government of the People's Republic of China and of the North Korean authorities of arms, ammunition and implements of war, atomic energy materials, petroleum, transportation materials of strategic value, and items useful in the production of arms, ammunition and implements of war;
(b) Determine which commodities exported from its territory fall within the embargo, and apply controls to give effect to the embargo;
(c) Prevent by all means within its jurisdiction the circumvention of controls on shipments applied by other States pursuant to the present resolution;
(d) Co-operate with other States in carrying out the purposes of this embargo;
(e) Report to the Additional Measures Committee, within thirty days and thereafter at the request of the Committee, on the measures taken in accordance with the present resolution.[30]

Nevertheless, one cannot ignore the fact that most Western states attempted to put off the imposition of sanctions for as long as possible.

Resolution 498 also succeeded in counteracting any Soviet

bloc allegations of American aggression in Korea. A determination by the General Assembly that the People's Republic of China was the state guilty of aggression ruled out the Communist charges that the guilt lay with the United States. The most lasting effect of the resolution, however, was on Communist China's hopes for admission to the United Nations. In fact, one of the major arguments used by the sponsors of the twelve-power resolution was that it would not indefinitely delay the admission of the People's Republic of China into the United Nations. The passage of the United States resolution effectively put off admission. Indeed, in the 1960s the consistent condemnation of South Africa led many African states to press for its expulsion on the grounds that a state condemned by the United Nations has no right to enter or remain in that organization. The People's Republic of China could not insist that it was a peace-loving state after having been condemned for aggression. In this area, therefore, the resolution had an immediate and devastating effect on Communist Chinese hope for UN membership. So strongly did the Communist Chinese feel about this resolution that they declared in the late 1960s, nearly twenty years after the passage of the resolution, that they would not enter the United Nations unless this resolution was publicly rescinded. (The fact that they did enter the United Nations in 1971 despite the failure of the General Assembly to rescind the resolution demonstrated a retreat on their part.)

Finally, UN action against the People's Republic of China consistently lowered UN prestige in the eyes of that state. The organization was pictured as a stooge of United States imperialism and was itself delegitimized. For example, on November 18, 1950, Kuo Mo-jo, head of the Communist Chinese delegation to the Second World Congress of Defenders of Peace in Warsaw, stated: "The American imperialists desecrate the U.N. By their criminally aggressive actions in Korea, they have turned the U.N. flag into a shameful rag. . . . The United Nations . . . has now become a screen behind which the aggressors violate peace. The U.N. Charter has become just so much paper." [31]

As a whole, then, resolution 498 had its most direct effect in the UN arena. It played an important part in defeating

Communist Chinese attempts to occupy the Chinese seat in the United Nations, and also laid the groundwork for the passage of resolution 500 in May 1951. In the international and domestic spheres resolution 498 was only a factor in the political conflict, and even here its influence was clearly limited. It failed to gain any new allies for the UN forces in Korea, but it did provide a partial justification for the American military build-up and protected the United Nations, to a large degree, from American public condemnation.

Resolutions 804 and 906 had more limited objectives and effects. Resolution 804 was essentially a reaction to the condition of some returning prisoners of war. The United States had several objectives in supporting this resolution. The primary one was to call world attention to Communist cruelty against defenseless prisoners of war, partially for propaganda purposes and partially to deter future mistreatment of prisoners of war. Also, several senators were pressuring the administration for more action on the reported atrocities and continued detention of many prisoners of war. On October 29, the United States Army War Crimes Division Report was released, undoubtedly in preparation for the presentation of the problem to the General Assembly the next day, but the charges that the Communists had murdered, tortured, starved, or otherwise mistreated at least 17,735 American and UN prisoners of war and 17,354 civilians created quite a stir.[32] The United States Senate was outraged, and Senator Mike Mansfield immediately requested information on what steps had been taken to punish the guilty parties.[33] Thus the situation was brought to the United Nations for domestic as well as international reasons, as a move in the political and psychological conflict between East and West. The resolution may also have been an emotional reaction to the feeling of helplessness on the part of the American government.

In any case, its effect on the treatment of the prisoners of war is unclear. Most prisoners had already been released by the time the resolution was passed, and the remainder would shortly follow; so it may have led to a slight improvement in the treatment of the prisoners of war who had not yet been released if the Communists wanted to counteract the propaganda effect of the resolution. However, from the United States' point of view resolution 804 was a psychological victory: it demonstrated Communist atrocities, was yet another factor in preventing the admission of Communist China into the United Nations, and may have diminished domestic pressure for action before the issue died down.

Resolution 906 had a more specific and limited objective— the release of eleven American airmen captured by the Communist Chinese; secondarily it was designed to pressure other states to increase their efforts for the release of these men. It did achieve those objectives; however, neither the direct appeal to the People's Republic of China nor the indirect appeal to other states succeeded in freeing the imprisoned airmen. Prime Minister Nehru of India reportedly asked the Indian ambassador to Peking to request the release of the American airmen, and Great Britain approached Asian states friendly to the People's Republic of China in order to gain their aid in this matter, but with disappointing results.[34] Premier Chou En-lai sharply criticized the resolution and asserted that the United Nations should have condemned the United States for sending the spies over China in the first place.[35] Then Peking radio said that neither threats nor UN condemnations could alter Communist China's right to deal with spies.[36]

The resolution had also requested that Secretary Dag Hammarskjöld "seek the release, in accordance with the Korean Armistice Agreement, of these eleven United Nations Command personnel, and all other captured personnel of the United Nations Command still detained." The Secretary General went to Peking, and on August 1, 1955, the People's Republic of China announced the release of the American airmen.[37]

Thus, resolution 906, the most limited and specific of the three condemnations issued against the People's Republic of China, achieved its primary objective, but only with the Secretary General's aid. The resolution was also successful, however, in easing some of the mounting domestic pressure concerning the detention of the airmen. Resolution 804 was in many ways a propaganda resolution, and in this respect it was successful, although its effect in improving the treatment of the prisoners

of war is in doubt. Resolution 498 was a vastly more complicated resolution with a variety of objectives. As we have seen,
some were successful, some not.

SOUTH AFRICA
Resolution 1805 (1962)

Although Portuguese navigators went ashore in South-West
Africa in the fifteenth and sixteenth centuries it was not until
the seventeenth century that periodic expeditions were made
there. In the beginning of the nineteenth century missionaries
settled in the territory, soon to be followed by traders and ex-
plorers. By the end of the century Germany had established its
authority over all of South-West Africa, built a railway line
and improved the harbor at Swakopmund, thus increasing immigration to the colony. In 1903 a revolt broke out among the
Bondelswarts of the South and shortly thereafter the Herero-
German War erupted, which lasted till 1906. With the outbreak
of World War I South African troops marched into the territory, and the outnumbered German forces surrendered on July
9, 1915. In the negotiations at Versailles it was decided to
place South-West Africa into the "C" category of mandates
under the League of Nations. South Africa would administer
the territory as the mandatory power under Article 22 of the
Covenant.

    (1) To those colonies and territories which as a con-
sequence of the last war have ceased to be under the
sovereignty of the States which formerly governed them and
which are inhabited by peoples not yet able to stand by themselves under the strenuous conditions of the modern world,
there should be applied the principle that the well-being and
development of such peoples form a sacred trust of civilization and that securities for the performance of this trust
should be embodied in this Covenant.
    (2) The best method of giving practical effect to this
principle is that the tutelage of such peoples should be
entrusted to advanced nations who by reason of their re-

sources, their experience or their geographical position can best undertake this responsibility, and who are willing to accept it, and that this tutelage should be exercised by them as Mandatories on behalf of the League. . . .

(6) There are territories, such as South-West Africa and certain of the South Pacific Islands, which, owing to the sparseness of their population or their small size, or their remoteness from the centres of civilization, or their geographical contiguity to the territory of the Mandatory, and other circumstances, can best be administered under the laws of the Mandatory as integral portions of its territory, subject to the safeguards above mentioned in the interests of the indigenous population.

(7) In every case of mandate, the Mandatory shall render to the Council an annual report in reference to the territory committed to its charge.

The permanent Mandates Commission received annual reports from South Africa as to the status of South-West Africa until 1945. Then at the first session of the UN General Assembly the South African delegate proposed the incorporation of South-West Africa into South Africa. The General Assembly rejected this proposal and recommended instead that South-West Africa be placed under the trusteeship system. South Africa refused on the grounds that it was not legally obliged to conclude a trusteeship agreement in place of the mandate and informed the General Assembly that it would continue to administer the territory in the spirit of the mandate. Thereafter, until 1947, South Africa voluntarily submitted reports describing the economic, social, and educational conditions of South-West Africa, but refused to recognize any supervisory jurisdiction of the United Nations. In 1947 the state decided that it would not submit any further information because the United Nations had made offensive use of the 1946 reports. In 1948 the General Assembly noted with regret that its recommendations as to placing South-West Africa under the trusteeship system had not been carried out, and requested that annual information be supplied on South-West Africa. In 1949 the General Assembly expressed regret that South Africa had failed to submit reports on South-West Africa for two years and recommended that reports be resumed.

The debate in this period attempted to resolve three questions: whether the mandate was still in force despite the expiration of the League of Nations; whether South Africa was under a legal obligation to enter into a trusteeship agreement; and whether South-West Africa was a non-self-governing territory under Chapter XI of the Charter. In December 1949 the General Assembly decided to submit the entire question to the International Court of Justice for an advisory opinion.

On July 11, 1950 the International Court of Justice delivered its advisory opinion. It declared that the mandate for South-West Africa was still in force; that the supervisory functions of the League of Nations were now to be exercised by the United Nations, to which annual reports and petitions were to be submitted; that South Africa was under an obligation to accept the jurisdiction of the International Court of Justice on the mandate; that South Africa was under no legal obligation to conclude a trusteeship agreement; and that the competence to modify the international status of South-West Africa rested with South Africa, acting with the assent of the United Nations.

The General Assembly approved resolution 449A on December 13, 1950, urging the government of the Union of South Africa "to take the necessary steps to give effect to the opinion of the International Court of Justice, including the transmission of reports on the administration of the Territory of South-West Africa and of petitions from communities or sections of the population of the Territory." The General Assembly further established a committee of five—Denmark, Syria, Thailand, the United States, and Uruguay—to confer with South Africa "concerning the procedural measures necessary for implementing the advisory opinion of the International Court of Justice." However, the General Assembly also reiterated its request to South Africa to place South-West Africa under the trusteeship system.

In 1951, the Ad Hoc Committee on South-West Africa reported that the Union of South Africa had submitted a proposal, which the Committee found unacceptable because it did not allow adequate UN supervision over the territory. The Ad Hoc Committee at that point submitted a counterproposal based on the Mandates Agreement that envisaged a League-of-Nations type supervision for the United Nations over South-

West Africa. South Africa replied that it was unwilling to accept the Ad Hoc Committee's proposal and refused to submit reports on the administration of the territory. Nevertheless, the General Assembly reappointed the Committee and requested that it continue to confer with the government of the Union of South Africa.

Between 1952 and 1954 the General Assembly passed a series of resolutions; these expressed regret that South Africa was unwilling to grant supervisory responsibilities to the United Nations and solemnly appealed for a reconsideration of its position; expressed its hope that South Africa would place South-West Africa under the international trusteeship system; recorded with deep regret that South Africa continued its refusal to implement the advisory opinion of the International Court of Justice in regard to South-West Africa; and noted with concern and further regret that South Africa had submitted neither reports nor petitions to the United Nations. During this period the General Assembly also established a Committee on South-West Africa, consisting of Brazil, Mexico, Norway, Pakistan, Syria, Thailand, and Uruguay, to examine reports and petitions from South-West Africa and transmit a report to the Secretary General.

In 1954 the General Assembly established rules of procedure for examining reports and petitions relating to South-West Africa; passed resolution 851, which noted that in several respects the administration of South-West Africa was not in conformity with the obligations under the mandate; reiterated its request that South Africa place South-West Africa under the trusteeship system; and approved five resolutions in reply to several petitions from South-West Africans, informing the petitioners of the 1950 opinion of the International Court of Justice. The General Assembly also reiterated what had now become an annual appeal that South Africa place South-West Africa under the international trusteeship system. This request was repeated in 1957, a year in which the General Assembly also noted that conditions in South-West Africa were still far from meeting the standards implicit in the mandate system, to say nothing of international trusteeship standards.

Meanwhile South Africa contended that the mandate on

South-West Africa had lapsed, so that its consequent failure to submit annual reports to the United Nations was justified. The General Assembly responded with resolution 1143, establishing a Good Offices Committee, consisting of the United States, the United Kingdom, and Brazil, to discuss with the South African government a "basis for an agreement which would continue to accord to the territory of South-West Africa an international status."

In 1958 the General Assembly reiterated its suggestion that South-West Africa be placed under the international trusteeship system but refused to accept the report of the Good Offices Committee on South Africa, which approved a South African plan for partition and partial annexation of the territory. The petitions received in the previous year were reviewed and the General Assembly again expressed its deep concern as to the social, economic, and political situation in the territory reported by the Committee on South-West Africa.

On November 17, 1959 the General Assembly approved a series of resolutions, which in addition to noting the South-West African petitions and reiterating its request to South Africa to place South-West Africa under the trusteeship system, became more specific—noting with concern and regret the South African removal of many natives from their land, especially from the Hoachanas Native Reserve, in order to make room for European settlers; considering the withdrawal of Hans Johannes Beukas's passport by the South African government an act of administration contrary to the mandate; noting with grave concern that the "administration of the Territory, in recent years, has been conducted increasingly in a manner contrary to the Mandate, the Charter of the United Nations, the Universal Declaration of Human Rights, the advisory opinions of the International Court of Justice, and the resolutions of the General Assembly"; and inviting the government of South Africa to enter into negotiations with the United Nations in order to place South-West Africa under the trusteeship system or to at least formulate proposals for administration in accordance with the mandate.

By 1960 the United Nations became more insistent and expressed its deep concern with the arbitrary imprisonment and deportation of South-West African leaders; requested the Food and Agriculture Organization, the World Health Organization, the UN Educational, Scientific, and Cultural Organization, and the UN Children's Fund to undertake programs "to assist the indigenous population of South-West Africa in their respective fields"; deplored the forceable removal of residents of the Windhoek Location to Katutura and expressed its deep regret concerning the murder of eleven Africans there; and deplored, deprecated, and disapproved of the policies (*apartheid* and others) practiced by South Africa in South-West Africa and requested a preliminary report on the implementation of this resolution from the Committee on South-West Africa.

In March and April of 1961 the General Assembly again noted with concern that South Africa had ignored UN resolutions, adopted a policy contrary to the Charter, and attempted to assimilate South-West Africa into South Africa; and in its resolution of April 7, 1961 called the attention of the Security Council to the situation in South-West Africa, declaring that it would endanger international peace and security if allowed to continue.

In December of the same year the General Assembly dissolved the Committee on South-West Africa; established a UN Special Committee for South-West Africa, consisting of Brazil, Burma, Mexico, Norway, the Philippines, Somaliland, and Togo, whose representatives were to visit South-West Africa and arrange for the release of all political prisoners, the evacuation of all South African military forces, the repeal of all racial laws and to prepare for general elections; and noted with the gravest concern, disappointment, and regret South Africa's continued suppression of the African population by laws and force and its refusal to heed UN resolutions.

There were several bases then, for resolution 1805: previous General Assembly resolutions, reports by special UN bodies, and petitions.

Resolution 1514 had called for a speedy end to colonialism since "all peoples have the right to self-determination"; resolution 1702 proclaimed "the inalienable right of the people of South-West Africa to independence and national sovereignty";

resolution 1761 deplored and deprecated South Africa's failure to heed previous UN resolutions by continuing its policy of *apartheid* and requested a partial boycott of South Africa. The report of the Special Committee on the Situation with regard to Implementation of the Declaration on the Granting of Independence to Colonial Countries and Peoples recommended "urgent, positive action, including the possibility of sanctions against South Africa, to prevent the annexation of South-West Africa and to ensure the emergence of South-West Africa into independence at the earliest date in accordance with the freely expressed wishes of the people." [1] The report of the Special Committee for South-West Africa recommended firm and decisive UN action such as ending the mandate and "assuming the administration of the territory to prepare its peoples for independence, if need be by imposing sanctions or employing other means to enforce compliance with its decisions or resolutions." [2]

Oral petitions presented by some of the leading members of the resistance organizations described the horrors of South African rule and suggested, among other actions, that the United Nations impose economic sanctions and use military force in order to enforce its decisions.

In the end, resolution 1805 was sponsored by 45 states. Of these, seven were original members (India, Iran, Iraq, Philippines, Saudi Arabia, Syria, and the United Arab Republic), fifteen were members admitted between 1945 and 1960 (Afghanistan, Burma, Cambodia, Ceylon, Ghana, Guinea, Indonesia, Jordan, Libya, Malaya, Morocco, Nepal, Pakistan, Sudan, and Tunisia), and 23 were admitted after 1960 (Algeria, Cameroon, Central African Republic, Chad, Congo [Brazzaville], Congo [Leopoldville], Dahomey, Gabon, Ivory Coast, Jamaica, Madagascar, Mali, Mauritania, Mongolia, Niger, Nigeria, Senegal, Sierre Leone, Somalia, Tanganyika, Togo, Uganda, Upper Volta). Thus, the majority of sponsors were states admitted after 1960, and with the exception of Jamaica all the sponsors were from the Afro-Asian group. Of these, two-thirds of the Asian and nearly 85 percent of the African group sponsored this resolution, which constituted nearly 78 percent of the entire Afro-Asian group.

The debate that preceded the approval of the resolution involved six steps, each of which was crucial to the final decision to condemn South Africa. First, before the discussion could even proceed, it had to be established that the United Nations had the right to consider this matter. South Africa argued that since the question of South-West Africa was under examination by the International Court of Justice, and the Court is a part of the United Nations, the rule of *sub judice* applied and the General Assembly could not discuss the case. The reply of the African states was strong and immediate. They questioned the applicability of the *sub judice* rule, contending that South Africa was using it to divert the General Assembly from its task of guaranteeing self-determination to South-West Africa. How could South Africa insist on the *sub judice* rule anyway, after refusing to be bound to the Court's opinions of 1950 and 1956? The African delegates agreed to postpone the entire discussion, in fact, if South Africa would agree to abide by any International Court decision on the Ethiopian-Liberian complaint then before the Court.

South Africa immediately replied that it had cooperated with the International Court of Justice by its very participation in the case and that it had not obeyed the 1950 opinion because at the time the Court had not had all the facts of the case. Had it had these facts the decision would have been different. Many Latin American states agreed with South Africa that General Assembly action should wait until the International Court reached a decision. Although they supported the African and Asian states in their attempt to have the United Nations revoke the mandate, they believed that such a move would have more effect if it had a firm legal foundation such as an International Court decision would provide.

The next step in UN consideration of the matter was to ascertain the facts of the case. Although all parties concerned agreed that the South African policy of *apartheid* had been extended to South-West Africa there was disagreement as to the underlying theory, effects, and implications of *apartheid*. South Africa insisted that *apartheid* was not meant to prevent the development of the black or Bantu peoples but gave to each population group the opportunity to develop at its own pace. The

Western members deplored *apartheid*, contending that it worked to the detriment of the Bantu population in South-West Africa. The African states were far more vociferous in their denunciation. The most moderate among them accused South Africa of using *apartheid* as a subterfuge for the organized exploitation of the African masses. Others went further and asserted that *apartheid* threatened the very existence of the black peoples. Yet others charged that the system was genocide in slow motion and that the Bantu population was being annihilated through torture and maltreatment. All agreed that South Africa was clearly violating Article 2 of the Mandate Agreement, that the "Mandatory shall promote to the utmost the material and moral well-being and the social progress of the inhabitants of the territory subject to the present Mandate." In addition, some African states claimed that South Africa was rapidly increasing its military potential and establishing military bases within the territory, thus violating Article 4 of the Mandate Agreement, that "no military or naval bases shall be established or fortifications erected in the territory." Others went even further and accused South Africa of sabotaging the UN operation in the Congo by supporting the forces fighting the United Nations.

South Africa denied the accusations of genocide and militarization. Its delegate pointed to the Joint Communiqué issued by the South African government and the chairman and vice-chairman of the Special Committee for South-West Africa, which had visited South-West Africa from May 9 to May 18, 1962. This communiqué declared that the chairman and vice-chairman had seen no evidence of militarization in South-West Africa during their visit and that they were satisfied with what they had seen. The two men had since repudiated the communiqué; however, South Africa used it in its defense. The African states insisted that the communiqué had been issued under duress, that the two men had had no freedom of movement and had seen only what the South African government wished them to see, and that there had been press censorship on part of this trip. South Africa countered that the two had been allowed to go anywhere they requested and had been satisfied with the itinerary prepared by the South African government. Only in one area had the number of newsmen accompanying them been restricted, and that because of particular difficulties in the terrain.

Although the African states believed that the facts were enough to indict and condemn South Africa, they felt that an exposé of South African intentions would be all the more damning. Therefore they proceeded to reveal what they believed were the true intentions of South Africa.

The African and Asian states claimed that South Africa wished to transform South-West Africa into a white-majority state and incorporate it, thus ending self-determination forever. Also, they said, South Africa was the keystone of an unholy alliance with Portugal and South Africa (later to include Southern Rhodesia) that was a threat to the African states.

This fear was encouraged by the Communist bloc, which claimed that South Africa was an aggressive imperialist power sharing with Portugal the aim of expanding northward in the African continent. This, together with South Africa's apparent militarization of the territory and suppression of its population, made the situation a threat and thus necessitated urgent action.

Another necessary step on the way to condemning a state is to prove that state's substantive guilt by determining its obligations and then considering whether the facts cited are in direct violation of those obligations. For this reason South Africa claimed that the mandate had ceased to exist along with the League of Nations, and that even if the mandate were still in existence, the United Nations had no supervisory power over it. Therefore, even if the African allegations were true, South Africa had not violated its obligations—and in any case the United Nations had no right to interfere. The African states countered that the 1950 advisory opinion of the International Court of Justice proved the mandate was still in existence; moreover, according to that opinion the United Nations had inherited the supervisory functions of the League of Nations and should therefore receive annual reports and petitions from the mandatory power. They further contended that if the mandate had indeed lapsed, South Africa no longer had legal authority over South-West Africa.

Once a majority of member states agreed that the United

Nations did have a role to play, and once most states agreed that South Africa had violated its obligations, it then remained to decide how the United Nations could ameliorate the situation. Most Western states insisted that the United Nations should do no more than admonish South Africa for its actions in South-West Africa. The Africans insisted that the United Nations revoke South Africa's mandate of South-West Africa and itself administer the territory. The Soviet bloc insisted not only on a revocation of the mandate but also on immediate self-determination for South-West Africa—or at least African (as opposed to UN) administration of the territory.

As it turned out, the final resolution was a significant retreat for the African states and went only one step beyond the suggestions of the Western powers. Sponsored by a majority of African states, resolution 1805 did not call for a revocation of the mandate but merely condemned "the continued refusal of the Government of South Africa to co-operate with the United Nations in the implementation of resolution 1702 (XVI) as well as other resolutions concerning South-West Africa." Since the Western states nevertheless objected to this resolution, the African states used several arguments in an attempt to gain their approval—first, that both *apartheid* and South Africa's actions in regard to South-West Africa had been condemned by most member states individually, so a resolution of condemnation would merely be a collective statement of what all had individually agreed to; second, that a condemnatory resolution would be an open appeal to the conscience of mankind which might make people the world over more aware of the evils of *apartheid,* especially within South-West Africa, perhaps creating a groundswell of public pressure that would force South Africa to change its policies; and third, that the United Nations could no longer ignore its obligations in the matter and must openly demonstrate its concern with the situation in South-West Africa. This could be done through an open and clear condemnation. The West countered that a resolution condemning South Africa would actually defeat its purpose by hardening the South African government's attitude and uniting its people behind its policies.

The final point considered was whether a condemnation

would enhance or diminish UN prestige. In considering the various options, the first concern, of course, was the effect that each might have on the achievement of the objective; but the second was the effect of the resolution and its consequences on the United Nations itself. Most Western states argued that since South Africa would not obey UN directives issued in the form of a condemnation, the United Nations would merely be demonstrating its impotence in this regard. A milder resolution might have more chance of implementation and even if not obeyed, would not so clearly demonstrate the futility of UN action in this area.

The African, Asian, and Communist states insisted that condemnation was the very least the United Nations could do in this case. South Africa had openly challenged the United Nations by refusing to comply with previous, milder General Assembly resolutions. Failure to condemn South Africa at this time would demonstrate that the United Nations was unwilling or unable to enforce its decisions, a fact that would cost it dear in prestige. These states insisted that a condemnation might have more effect than previous resolutions—and in any case it was better for the United Nations to shatter on the rock of principle than to dissipate in the waters of compromise.

Between 1962 and 1970 the United Nations became more vociferous in its condemnation of South Africa for its actions in South-West Africa. On October 27, 1966 the General Assembly passed resolution 2145 (XXI), terminating South Africa's mandate and transferring responsibility for South-West Africa to the United Nations. Thereafter, the resolutions became ever stronger in the face of South Africa's continuing refusal to obey General Assembly and, later, Security Council directives.

Throughout this period sentiment shifted toward the African position. The Latin American states still officially urged caution and moderation, but by 1970 they routinely voted with the Afro-Asian group on South-West African matters. In addition, many Western European states moved toward the African position, although some argued for modification in the debate. Even on resolutions they could not support, most Western states abstained rather than openly vote in opposition. Only

South Africa and Portugal consistently voted against these resolutions. Thus, the African states went from achieving a large
majority to achieving near-unanimity in their South-West African resolutions.

The Soviet bloc, although supporting the African resolutions,
continued to insist on immediate independence for South-West
Africa.

The debates during this period generally followed the same
pattern: South Africa continued to contest the very legality of
UN consideration of the South-West Africa matter, especially
after the International Court decided in July 1966 that Ethiopia and Liberia had no legal right to question the mandatory's
performance of its obligations. South Africa considered this a
reversal of the Court's opinions of 1950 and 1956 and em-
phasized their contention that the United Nations had no right
to discuss the matter by absenting itself from all committee
meetings devoted to South-West Africa.

As to the facts of the case, South Africa insisted that because
it had presented conclusive evidence to the contrary, Ethiopia and Liberia no longer accused the state of intentionally
oppressing the Bantu population in South-West Africa, but said
instead that South African policies violated an international human rights norm of nondiscrimination, a much weaker charge.
South Africa claimed this as proof that the original charges
were false. The African states insisted, however, that the plea
had not been changed in the International Court of Justice,
that South Africa was guilty of oppression and maltreatment
of the natives, and that the very presence of South African
personnel in South-West Africa after revocation of the mandate
was aggression and a threat to international peace and security.
South Africa had an obligation to leave the territory and allow
the United Nations to take jurisdiction over it. Since it refused
to leave voluntarily, the United Nations had to find a means
to force it to obey General Assembly resolution 2145 (XXI).
Several types of sanctions were recommended, particularly economic and military, and the General Assembly condemned
those states that continued to trade with and supply arms to
South Africa while condemning South Africa for its South-
West Africa policy.

The West felt that the entire series of condemnations and suggestions of sanctions diminished the prestige of the United Nations; the African states claimed that UN prestige would sink even lower if it allowed South Africa to openly flout its directives, whereas its prestige could only be increased if the Western states would cooperate in applying economic sanctions and in pressuring South Africa to withdraw from South-West Africa.

In the voting that followed, resolution 1805 (XVII) was adopted 96 to 0 with one abstention in the Fourth Committee and 96 to 2 in the General Assembly. All UN members voted for the resolution in the Fourth Committee except for Portugal, which abstained, and El Salvador, Iceland, Laos, Luxembourg, Madagascar, Nicaragua, Paraguay, Peru, Rwanda, Saudi Arabia, South Africa, Upper Volta, and Yemen, which did not participate in the vote. South Africa did not participate because it felt that the *sub judice* rule made the entire discussion illegal.

The resolution adopted was not identical to the original draft. The Soviet bloc had pressed for a more authoritarian resolution, but withdrew its amendments when the sponsors, together with four other states, presented a revised resolution. This deleted the word *full* from what had been "full implementation of General Assembly resolution 1702" in paragraph 2; inserted in operative paragraph 3 the phrase *mutatis mutandis* between the words "to discharge" and "the tasks assigned to the Special Committee"; in the same paragraph the words "the General Assembly *at its present or* at its eighteenth session"; and the word "*Resident* United Nations Technical Assistance." The United States had attempted to modify the resolution considerably, but both its amendments were rejected in the voting.

Despite the frustration of years of futile resolutions, there are several general reasons for African pressure to condemn South Africa as severely as possible. Few states expect South Africa to grant South-West Africa independence, but many hope that South Africa will at least heed UN resolutions to the extent that they will not implement repressive legislation.[3] If UN resolutions should achieve even part of their goal they could be deemed successful. And even if South Africa remained adamant, these resolutions might have the indirect effect of causing internal dissension within South Africa. They could foster disagreement among the comparatively united white community by widening the existing rift between the more moderate English-speaking population and the Afrikaans-speaking population, which is far more extreme on the question of South-West Africa.[4] The English-speaking population might then press for changes to make the South-West African situation more acceptable and thus reduce world pressure on South Africa. Or a series of condemnations might encourage the Bantu population of South Africa and South-West Africa in their struggle to alter the system by which they are governed.[5] In the same way, the continuing resolutions would legitimize the liberation movements in South-West Africa.[6] The recognition accorded petitioners and given them by other processes associated with the passage of a UN resolution might boost the morale of these freedom-fighters and thereby increase their chances for eventual victory. It could also enhance their stature in the eyes of other states, thus increasing the possibilities of actual material aid to these movements.

Even if these resolutions did not affect South Africa itself, either directly or indirectly, they were only one segment of the struggle for South-West Africa's freedom, an attempt to carry the struggle into the diplomatic sphere. If the attempt to isolate South Africa should succeed, South Africa would become a pariah among nations and no state would be willing to be associated or identified with it.[7] This universal ostracism might finally convince South Africa of the error of its ways.

The diplomatic isolation of South Africa would also affect its allies. Strong measures such as condemnatory resolutions or those advocating sanctions or expulsion from the UN would attract the greatest publicity in the Western states and arouse public support there.[8]

Since most African states have had some colonial experience, they share an abhorrence of its effects and a fear that it may return in a new guise, such as economic or neo-colonialism. It is therefore quite natural that they seek to eliminate the remnants of colonialism. South Africa's colonial move in regard to South-West Africa is particularly galling to the African states because of the very principle underlying the South African policy of *apartheid*. Having recently emerged from colonialism, the African states are now seeking to assert their equality with all states. This striving for equality takes on all the aspects of a moral crusade.[9] "No African country or nation is really free until all Africa is free," said Addis Ababa in 1963. UN condemnations of South Africa, both for its policy toward South-West Africa and for its *apartheid* system, are a reaffirmation of this principle of equality, which the colonial states in general and South Africa in particular have so gravely violated.

Also, consider the internal situation of these states. Since the composition and borders of most African states have been determined by their colonial masters, not by their indigenous needs, there is little common loyalty or sense of identity within these states. Many individuals retain a greater loyalty to their tribe, which may be divided among two or three states, than to the state in which they actually reside. These states are artificial concepts, and a sense of loyalty and unity must be created if they are to survive as viable entities.[10] Opposition to an external enemy is often the most useful unifying element, and in this sense African leaders use South Africa, at least partially, for their own ends. To go one step further, if there were no South Africa, the African leaders might very well have had to invent one.

A second internal element influencing foreign policy toward South Africa is the inherent instability of the African leadership. In most states there is a budding opposition of educated young leaders who wish to gain power. In addition, the military is always standing in the wings, ready to take power if the present government should fail. Both groups, as well as many lesser officials and members of the informed public, pressure governmental leaders for action on the colonial issue.[11] Action in the United Nations partially satisfies these demands and may help to stem the growing sense of frustration felt by these individuals.[12]

A final contributing factor to the condemnations of South Africa for its South-West African policy is the very existence of the United Nations. The United Nations is a public forum in which all states can air their grievances. This provides an emotional outlet for the leaders of African states, an arena in which they can react publicly to South African provocations.[13] Because this satisfies their need for some sort of action, the United Nations can be said to act as a balm for their collective conscience.

Salving the collective conscience is the beginning of a gradually accelerating process. As the African states compete with each other in expressing loyalty to their African brethren and opposition to colonialism, each state becomes more vociferous.[14] Thus the entire African bloc is trapped in its rhetoric and forced to propose progressively stronger resolutions against South Africa.[15] The tone of the group is set by its most radical members since, in the name of bloc solidarity, the more moderate members support most resolutions the extremists propose. This becomes a measure of radicalism and thus a source of competition among the African states. In addition, the very fact that earlier resolutions have gone unheeded forces the United Nations itself to acquiesce in more severe resolutions. Since the United Nations cannot indefinitely repeat the same resolutions it must either drop the subject entirely or make the resolutions progressively stronger.[16] As the subject becomes the focus of world attention it cannot be dismissed from the international arena. So in a sense the United Nations is part of a perpetual motion machine.

There are two other reasons for the continual passage of condemnatory resolutions against South Africa. First, since the United Nations has delegitimized the use of force in international conflicts, the African states use these resolutions as a relegitimization of the use of force in the North-South conflict. This is due to the African interpretation of the UN Charter, which gives priority to human rights over the peaceful settlement of disputes.[17]

The founders of the United Nations had assumed that the primary function of the organization would be peacekeeping, as indicated in the preamble and the statement of purposes and principles (Articles 1 and 2). But the African states believe the United Nations should turn its major efforts to the eradication of colonialism; they insist that human rights are the essential purpose of the organization and peace is only secondary.[18] If human rights and peace conflict then violence becomes legitimate in order to remove the violation of human rights.

Thus in the event that the African states gain enough power in the future to militarily overthrow the South African government, they want to have the near-unanimous approval of the UN organization for this use of force.

Second, every UN resolution acts as a basis for a stronger resolution if the first is not implemented. Thus a resolution deploring South African action toward South-West Africa lays the groundwork for a resolution that condemns the same action, while an accumulation of condemnatory resolutions prepares for the eventual expulsion of or utilization of sanctions against South Africa.

It can be readily seen from this that UN condemnations are generally not the result of one or two actions that enrage the collective conscience of mankind, but stem rather from a wide variety of contributing factors. The overt act plays a major part in bringing about the condemnation, but the contributing factors are the characteristics and history of the condemning states themselves, and the very nature of the UN organization that encourages condemnations in such cases.

The African population was at first encouraged by UN resolutions condemning South Africa, then disillusioned as the lack of positive effects became manifest.[19] As a result, some of the festering anger was directed at the United Nations as its inefficacy became clear. Mr. Garoeb, speaking on behalf of the South-West African People's Organization (SWAPO) stated:

> If it came to the use of force, the rest of the Member states should use whatever military power they possessed to implement the United Nations resolution. By doing so, they would not only fulfill their sacred obligation towards the people of Namibia, but such action would also enhance the prestige of the United Nations. The greatest threat to the existence of the United Nations was its inability to implement its own resolutions.[20]

Along with their increasing sense of frustration with the United Nations, awareness grew among the African population that South-West Africans had to take direct action if they were ever to achieve independence. In March 1966 the first group of guerrillas infiltrated across the border into South-West Africa, and from then on, there were sporadic outbreaks of fighting between South-West African police and the guerrillas.

On the other hand, it seemed to the European population that UN action in this arena was provoking resentment and hostility and consolidating support for the government in South-West Africa. Before 1961 the United Nations had not directly condemned South Africa for its actions in South-West Africa; by March 30, 1966, South Africa had been condemned several times. In 1966, the Nationalist Party of South-West Africa, affiliated with the Nationalist Party of South Africa, increased its percentage of the vote from approximately 59.3 percent in 1961 to 67.7 percent, winning a landslide decision in the general elections, capturing all six seats allotted to South-West Africa in the South African House of Assembly and all eighteen seats in the territorial Legislative Assembly.[21] The United National South-West Party percentage, on the other hand, decreased from about 40.6 percent in 1961 to 32.2 percent in 1966. The implications of UN pressure on South Africa were not lost on the opposition. The leader of the United Party, Sir de Villiers Graaf, stated:

> We have objected firmly to outside interference because we realize that not only will it assist the Government to chase the electors into just one *kraal,* which they are desperately trying to do, but we realize also that it will interfere with our opportunities of getting rid of this Government and arriving at a sound solution in South Africa.[22]

Within South Africa itself, the reaction to UN condemnations was also largely negative. Even the opposition United Party backed the National Party against the United Nations. And Sir de Villiers Graaf stated in November 1967: "There was grave unrest in the world and the United Nations had obviously failed to keep the peace. The organization suffered from a highly unbalanced obsession with South Africa."[23] He further said that any attempt to influence South Africa by threats of violence or by terrorist incursions would meet the united opposition of all South Africans. This national unity was also stressed by a Nationalist member of Parliament, Mr. B. Coetzee: "Anybody who knows anything about psychology knows that when a nation is involved in a struggle for survival, the more pressure one brings to bear on the nation, the more one unites the masses, the more one drives them into one camp." [24]

So intense was the resentment of South Africans against the United Nations that the gravest charge leveled by one party against the other was that it was giving in to international pressure and harkening to the voice of world public opinion. In the debates in Parliament, being "soft on the United Nations" was the unpardonable offense.

A further indication of the possible effects of UN condemnatory resolutions on the South African population has been the rate of emigration. In 1962, the year following the first overt condemnation of South Africa, emigration fell by about 40 percent. The following year, after a second condemnatory resolution, emigration again fell by about 20 percent. In the years following, the rate of emigration increased by slightly more than 10 percent each year, but in 1968 it fell slightly and in 1969 it had again fallen by approximately 10 percent. During the late 1960s emigration never reached the level of the peak years 1960 and 1961, when South Africa was not condemned.

In measuring the effects of these resolutions on the South African government, one must clearly distinguish between the government's basic primary responsibilities and its long-range political goals. In its primary responsibilities the South African government did not make any attempt to compromise with the United Nations. It moved firmly to crush all guerrilla movements in South-West Africa, and has continued to arrest guerrillas, potential guerrillas, and the political leaders of the guerrilla movement.

In the political field South African action has not been quite so direct and forceful. South Africa virtually ignores most UN resolutions, refuses to expend any effort to prevent or modify these resolutions, and often absents itself from committee meetings that discuss South-West Africa. The government rarely comments on these resolutions and denounces only the most extreme ones, thus demonstrating that the resolutions have no discernible effects on its policy. Yet while South Africa denies any UN jurisdiction, it does try to counter UN claims and resolutions. For example, *South-West Africa Survey, 1967*, published and transmitted to the United Nations, was an attempt to explain the progress of South-West Africa and offset any harmful effects of UN condemnatory resolutions.

> There was nothing to hide; and with a view to creating better understanding . . . South Africa would on a voluntary basis furnish all information of its policies and of the progress made in their application, not only in the Republic but also in South-West Africa.
>
> The Survey set out to give a picture in fair detail of the situation as it affects the more important spheres of life, so that the reader may appreciate the unremitting and by no means unsuccessful efforts which have been made in difficult circumstances to do the best possible for all the Territory's peoples, in leading them to self-determination and stable self-realization.[25]

Shortly thereafter, in response to UN resolution 2440 (XXIII) condemning South Africa's alleged mistreatment of prisoners in 1968, the Foreign Affairs Department of South Africa in 1969 published *Prison Administration in South Africa.*

> For the last fifty years the South African prison authorities have been in constant touch with prison administrations abroad and with academicians and experts at home to ensure that South Africa keeps abreast of new developments in prison techniques and that the latest proven methods are employed in its prisons. In this way South Africa has been able to adapt the ideas of leading world experts to local conditions, and to evolve a penal system which measures up to the highest standards.
>
> South Africa's present penal legislation, based on international standards adopted by the 1955 United Nations Congress on the Prevention of Crime and the Treatment of Offenders, speaks for itself.[26]

A special chapter in this monograph was devoted to an exposé of attempts to discredit the South African prison system.

Finally, in 1971, in response to continued UN criticism, South Africa published a booklet describing Ovamboland and the progress it had made under South Africa's tutelage.

The Owambo enjoy a considerable degree of autonomy and have achieved gratifying progress in most of the important human activities. The South African Government looks forward to the day when the Owambo nation will take its rightful position alongside the other nations of Southern Africa.[27]

Owambo has made good progress . . . against a background of climatic and geographical disadvantages. The progress achieved to date is obviously due in large measure to Owambo's special relationship with South Africa. South Africa's support cannot be measured in money alone, though this is considerable. More important are the facilities and services which South Africa provides, including transport services, harbours, telecommunications, trained personnel, and in general technical expertise. In aspects of administration, and in the scientific and technical fields, the country and its people can rely on staff with intimate experience of local conditions and of the best solutions to particular problems. In many respects, South Africa's contribution is irreplaceable and Owambo's progress on the road to self-determination is dependent on her present natural relationship with South Africa remaining undisturbed.[28]

On the other hand, concessions such as South Africa's failure to annex the Territory of South-West Africa are without question due to UN pressure. And increased UN attention may also have prevented South African implementation of more repressive legislation in the territory.

Despite its show of indifference, South Africa has indeed reacted overtly to the United Nations on the issue of South-West Africa. On May 10, 1961, it offered to invite an independent person of international standing, subject to agreement of the United Nations and the South African government, to conduct an impartial inquiry into the situation in South-West Africa; and shortly thereafter, South Africa offered to invite three past presidents of the General Assembly to determine whether there was any threat to international peace and security in South-West Africa, or whether South Africa was militarizing the territory or exterminating the native population.[29]

In addition, UN condemnations, along with other forms of international censure, can be said to be partially responsible for the compromise solution proposed by the Odendaal Commission formed by the South African government in 1962. The Odendaal Report, presented to the South African House of Assembly on January 27, 1964, suggested dividing South-West Africa into eleven regions, ten nonwhite and one white. Its general acceptance by the government can only reflect the state's need to find some compromise, a *modus vivendi,* with the United Nations. After their 1946 attempt to annex South-West Africa had been rejected by the General Assembly, South African leaders feared the consequences of openly incorporating South-West Africa, yet were extremely reluctant to grant full independence to this mineral-rich territory. Partition would satisfy world pressure for self-determination, rid South Africa of half a million Bantu, and allow it to retain much of the mineral resources. The idea of partition was presented to the Good Offices Committee on South-West Africa in 1958, but the General Assembly rejected it in resolution 1243 (XIII). Yet South Africa considered this plan to be the best compromise, and for this reason the Odendaal Commission was formed and its report accepted.

Within the South African Parliament the opposition often charged that the Odendaal Report was a concession to world opinion. The government strongly denied this, yet their pointing out that the opposition plan for a federated South-West Africa consisting of just two parts, North and South, would not have satisfied the United Nations does suggest that the plan was adopted as a compromise with international opinion, as symbolized by the UN resolutions. Thus Prime Minister Verwoerd answered when confronted with such charges from the United and Progressive parties:

> In suggesting a separation between the north and the south, are the Opposition not going to come into conflict with the United Nations in the same way as the Arden-Clarke Commission did and in the same way that our policy, according to them, will be rejected by the United Nations? Will the plans put forward by the United Party put a stop to the agitation against South Africa? . . . Inherently the

solution that we put forward satisfies all these demands
which have been formulated in the council chambers of the
world.[30]

An additional indication of the attempt to reconcile the South
African policy with the United Nations has been the continual
assertion that no other state, not even the United Nations, could
do as much for South-West Africa as South Africa has done.
On this point both parties agree.

> No other country, not even U.N., could do more for the
> well-being of the inhabitants of South-West, of all races
> and colours, than South Africa can do. It is a false accusa-
> tion which is being made overseas that the bulk is being
> given to Whites and only illusions to the non-Whites. (Prime
> Minister Verwoerd) [31]
> South Africa has in fact done as good a job in carrying
> out the mandate over South-West Africa as has been done
> by any other mandatory in respect of the various territories
> which were placed under the mandate. (Mr. Tuker, United
> Party) [32]
> The Prime Minister and the Government are going to
> continue to build up South-West Africa, to govern it in
> terms of the mandate, and to make it a happy and econom-
> ically prosperous territory. (Mr. B. Coetzee, National
> Party) [33]

Indeed, the very fact that South Africa was willing to spend
over R60,000,000 (as recommended in the Odendaal Report)
on the development of the nonwhite population is an indication, not of altruism, but of a definite response to the condemnatory resolutions. Condemnations have therefore improved the
lot of the nonwhite population by forcing South Africa to spend
more money on them than it would have done had it been left
to its own devices.

> I should like to remind the hon. member that his leader
> and his party embraced the Bantusan policy because they
> wanted peace in the face of United Nations attacks, and
> the hon. member for Constantia (Mr. Waterson) pointed
> out tonight how there may very well be truth in the allega-
> tion that this vast amount of money, approximately
> R200,000,000 is being spent to appease world opinion. (Mr.
> Thompson, United Party) [34]

South Africa went even further in announcing a five-year plan for the development of South-West Africa with a large portion devoted to the Bantu sectors. A large hydroelectric scheme was also proposed.[35]

In response to Security Council resolution 309 (1972), South Africa invited the Secretary General to visit South-West Africa, and following this visit, the South African Foreign Minister visited the Secretary General in New York. South Africa confirmed then that its policy toward South-West Africa was one of self-determination and independence and agreed to accept and cooperate with a special representative of the Secretary General to facilitate that aim. In March 1967 South Africa had announced an offer of self-determination to the Owambos; now the state announced a timetable for granting further autonomy to Ovamboland. A new Owambo legislature was to be elected and full self-rule implemented in 1973.

An additional reaction to international pressure was evident in South Africa's frantic search for friends. For example, it offered foreign aid and technical expertise to the African states if they would end their hostility.

Finally, UN condemnations, together with growing international hostility, have forced South Africa to vastly increase its expenditures for modernization and expansion of its armed forces and to become nearly self-sufficient in arms production. In 1960–1961, 0.9 percent of its gross national product or 6.6 percent of its total expenditure was devoted to defense. This increased to 2.4 percent of the gross national product in 1969-1970 or 16.1 percent of total state expenditure.[36] According to a government White Paper, these expenditures were made necessary because of ever-increasing foreign threats. UN condemnatory resolutions, as a partial reflection of this hostility, thus contributed to the growing feeling of insecurity that led to larger defense expenditures.

The increase in hostility is also reflected in the vast efforts and expenditures devoted to making South Africa self-sufficient, action taken in fear of an effective arms embargo. In 1966 a former Minister of Defense told the Nationalist Party Congress at Windhoek that he had brought from Europe 128 licenses for the manufacture of armaments in South Africa. South Af-

rica was building its own jet trainers, and "from a .22 cartridge
to the newest in armoured vehicles, from the smallest item to
the latest in bombs—today everything can be manufactured
locally." [37]

The effects of the condemnations on the allies of South Africa, the Western states, must be assessed indirectly. There are
neither public opinion polls on this subject in the Western
states, nor do governments readily divulge their correspondence
and messages to other states. However, statistics on trade, foreign investment, tourism, and immigration will usually indicate the status of a state's relationship with other states,
especially with its allies. Statistics relating to arms trade in
particular can be useful to examine since a state that is unfriendly to another will certainly not sell it arms. Foreign trade
and investment express the confidence of the population at
large as well as that of large corporations in the stability and
viability of a state. And since trade often involves credit, participation necessitates some confidence in a government's future stability. Tourism also indicates confidence in a state's
viability. If the area is considered unstable or unfriendly, few
tourists will come to visit. Furthermore, governments often discourage tourism to these areas. Shortly prior to the June 1967
Mideast war, for example, the United States State Department
banned all travel to any of the belligerents in the area. In the
same way, many African states will not allow South African
citizens to enter their states unless they expressly denounce
apartheid, and many Arab states refuse to allow Jews to enter
their territory. It is only with détente that tourism increases.
To a certain extent immigration, in cases where residents are
not driven across the border, also reflects a degree of confidence by the general population and a general lack of belligerence on the part of their governments.

Along with most UN members, the Western states condemn
South Africa's action in South-West Africa. Yet some of the
West's actions belie this posture. In the arena of world trade,
especially military trade, France has continued to sell arms to
South Africa despite a UN arms embargo.[38] On July 20, 1970,
Secretary Douglas-Home announced that Great Britain would

consider the sale of arms to South Africa for maritime defense.[39] On the other hand, the United States imposed an arms embargo on South Africa in January 1965,[40] but firmly refused to order a trade embargo on that state. In fact, there has been a steady increase in trade. Whereas in 1960 South Africa imported R1,111,300,000 worth of goods and exported R884,000,000 worth of goods (excluding gold), by 1969 these figures had reached R2,048,200,000 worth of imports and R1,471,000,000 worth of exports (excluding gold). The main trading partners by far are the Western states. And despite some fluctuations, Western foreign investments in South Africa show a continual upward trend. Since much of this investment is made by governments it indicates that there has been a steady increase in financial support of South Africa despite official condemnations. In addition, investments by the private sector indicate confidence in the stability and viability of South Africa in its present form. So UN condemnations have had little or no effect on foreign investments in South Africa.

During this period tourism to South Africa also showed a steady, consistent gain. Much of this tourism came from the white Southern African states, yet a growing proportion came from Western Europe and North America. There were 166,111 tourists from Southern Africa in 1962 and 192,070 in 1968, which is about a 15 percent increase. From other areas of the world, however, there were only 36,057 tourists in 1962, but 107,702 in 1968—a threefold increase.[41] Considering the travel distance between South Africa and Western Europe or North America, this represents a strong demonstration of confidence not at all undermined by UN condemnations.

Finally, since 1963 there has been an average of about 40,000 immigrants per year, as compared to an emigration rate of about 10,000, a net gain in the white population of about 30,000 annually. This consistency would indicate that UN condemnations have had little effect on the faith, or lack of faith, in the continued viability of South Africa on the part of immigrants and emigrants respectively. Generally, most of this immigration is from Western countries; less than 25 percent comes from white minorities in African states. In 1968, for example, out of 40,548 immigrants, only 8,910 came from other African states, while 29,437 came from Europe, 808 from America, 440 from Asia, and 953 from Australia, New Zealand, and other states.[42] It is important to note that since the majority of immigrants did not come from neighboring African states they were not forced to come to South Africa but did so of their own free will, thereby demonstrating confidence in the country's stability. In fact, in 1962, the year following the first condemnation of South Africa, immigration increased by 22 percent. In 1963, following a second condemnation, it increased by 45 percent. One may safely assume, then, that UN condemnations had little effect on the rate of immigration.

The process of condemnations did create some friction between the Western states and South Africa, which felt betrayed by its allies who participated in its condemnation. In addition, the Western allies applied diplomatic pressure on South Africa to compromise its stand on the South-West African issue. This friction was intensified by the arms embargo.

UN activity also damaged relations between South Africa and some small neutral states. For example, South Africa became increasingly incensed by Israeli statements and votes in the United Nations. On November 19, 1961, Prime Minister Verwoerd stated that the Israeli policy in the United Nations was a tragedy for South African Jewry and in light of this policy, South Africa might adopt a new line toward Israel.[43] Three days later he accused Israel of utterly deplorable action in the United Nations and said that Israel itself was an *apartheid* state.[44] He then accused Israel of voting the way it did in the United Nations for business rather than moral reasons.

On September 29, 1963, South Africa asserted that Israel's failure to send a new diplomatic representative to South Africa would only hurt Israel, for the next time Israel was in difficulty, South Africa would refuse aid. On May 30, 1968 Foreign Minister Mueller chided Israel for its unfavorable remarks about South Africa in the United Nations and hinted at a withdrawal of the South African diplomatic mission in Israel.[45]

UN condemnatory resolutions also helped to legitimize the resistance movements in South-West Africa. For example, previously neutral states, such as the Scandinavian ones, were able to aid the resistance movements with the backing and authority of the United Nations. Such legitimization and consequent aid is of great consequence to any resistance movement.

Finally, South Africa has attempted to break the solid front of African states aligned against it. Diplomatic relations were established with Malawi in September 1967.[46] And South Africa has made overtures to Botswana, Lesotho, and Swaziland as well as to other African states such as Madagascar, Mauritania, the Ivory Coast, Ghana, Dahomey, Niger, Gabon, and Rwanda.[47] Indeed, some of these states began moving toward a more moderate position in the hope that persuasion would accomplish what threats could not. This suggests that some of these states believed condemnations alone would not accomplish their purpose.

UN condemnations had a further effect on South Africa's position in the international arena. In effect, they reflected world condemnation, and they precipitated a stream of condemnations from other international organizations.

On March 15, 1961, South Africa withdrew from the Commonwealth. On July 15, 1963 Prime Minister Verwoerd announced that South Africa would withdraw from the UN Economic Commission for Africa because of the hostility of the African states; two weeks later it was suspended from that organization by the Economic and Social Council. On March 11, 1964, South Africa withdrew from the International Labour Organization, and several days later it walked out of the World Health Organization Annual Assembly.[48]

South Africa was barred from the Olympic Games of 1964 and 1968, and in 1970 it was banned from the Olympic movement. It has been suspended by the International Football Federation, and its athletes have been barred from international organizations for amateur boxing and wrestling, basketball, fencing, and table tennis.[49]

The Inter-Parliamentary Union and Amnesty International attacked South Africa's *apartheid* policy in 1965, and UNESCO published a report on *apartheid* in 1967.[50] Two years before this the carrier *Independence* canceled a visit to South Africa. South Africa has been expelled or suspended or has withdrawn from the following international organizations: UNESCO, the Commission for Technical Cooperation in Africa, the Scientific

Council for Africa, the International Civil Aviation Organization, the International Telecommunications Union, the Food and Agriculture Organization, and the Congress of the Universal Postal Union. Further, the World Council of Churches and the Vatican have indicated their strong disapproval of South Africa's policies.[51]

The immediate effect of resolution 1805 itself was to set a pattern for future resolutions on South-West African policy. After its passage condemnations followed each other in rapid succession: Two in 1963; one in 1965; one in 1966; two in 1967; and one each in 1968 and 1969. Several other resolutions were also introduced that censured South Africa for *apartheid* in South-West Africa or, in conjunction with other colonialist states, for refusing to grant to their colonies the right of self-determination. These condemnations became progressively more severe. Whereas resolution 1805 only condemned the country's policies, later resolutions condemned the government itself, which is far graver. The same was true of Security Council resolutions.

These resolutions led to proposals for further measures such as sanctions and expulsion. (In its 1974 session, the General Assembly did suspend South Africa.) Indeed resolution 1899 in 1963 requested an arms and petroleum embargo, a request to which many members responded favorably. (Most of the states favoring this resolution had already stopped trading with South Africa; on the other hand, most of the remainder, including the United States and Canada, refused to impose an embargo merely because of this resolution.) These condemnations led to the inevitable termination of the South-West African mandate on October 27, 1966 in resolution 2145 (XXI) South-West Africa was declared under UN jurisdiction and any further occupation constituted "a grave threat to international peace and security" (resolution 2372). South Africa had gradually come to a point where it was ignoring all but the most severe resolutions, and it was only with the passage of resolution 2145 terminating the mandate that Prime Minister Verwoerd as well as the Minister for Foreign Affairs felt called upon to publicly denounce it.

> All we ever ask the world and ask anew is to leave us alone. We will solve our own problems in our own time and in our own way. . . . We will continue to administer South-West Africa as we have always done and we will carry out what has been planned, taking into account the demands of the times. (Prime Minister Verwoerd)
>
> We must . . . also be prepared to withstand mandatory sanctions, and the world may as well know that the Government is already taking steps to meet this eventuality. (Foreign Minister) [52]

In the early days of the United Nations a condemnation was a relatively rare and rather extreme measure. It was the subject of discussions, articles, editorials, and banner headlines, as the most important news of the day. Gradually, however, the shock wore off, condemnations became routine, and the entire concept of UN condemnations as an expression of universal moral opprobrium gradually diminished in value. In fact, each resolution makes it clearer that the United Nations condemns because it can do nothing else. This has led to a devaluation of the United Nations, not only in the eyes of South Africa, but in those of the Africans themselves as well as in the eyes of neutral observers. Thus the South African Prime Minister has stated that "the United Nations has become our Cuba," [53] and in 1966 the South-West African leaders decided to take up arms because of their loss of confidence in the efficacy of UN actions.

> We can only accept full and total independence for Namibia now. The resolve to take up arms in 1966 came after the let-down by the international community. We want to emphasize that we will continue to fight for our freedom where international action leads to no results, until we have achieved independence. (Mr. Nujoma, SWAPO) [54]

And the Mexican representative to the UN warned that

> My delegation therefore fears that as far as South West Africa is concerned, having adopted a resolution with an exaggerated degree of unanimity, resolution 2145 (XXI), we are now wandering off along the deceptive road of high-sounding resolutions devoid of any real content, resolutions

that become ever more dangerous in that they cut the Organization off from the real possibilities for political action and consequently diminish its prestige. (Mr. Cuevas Cancino, Mexico) [55]

Nevertheless, UN condemnatory resolutions do seem to have had some effect on South Africa. The state has made certain concessions, however small and unsatisfactory to the country's critics, on the South-West African question, and they must be recognized as concessions to the United Nations.

ISRAEL
Resolution 256 (1968)

In 1897 the first World Zionist Congress declared as its objective the establishment of a Jewish "homeland in Palestine secured by public law." The movement grew and gradually gained enough momentum and adherents for the British government to feel it expedient to provide support. On November 2, 1917 the British government issued the Balfour Declaration, which stated: "His Majesty's Government views with favour the establishment in Palestine of a national home for the Jewish people and will use their best endeavors to facilitate the achievement of this object." On July 22, 1922 Great Britain was formally confirmed as mandatory power over Palestine, the mandate expressly providing for a Jewish state in Palestine. But Arab opposition to the plan, increased Jewish immigration after the ascent of Hitler, and British need for Arab support in the coming war led finally to the British government's publication of the White Paper of 1939, providing for a five-year restriction on, and subsequent cessation of, Jewish immigration into this area.

In 1943, with the war moving away from the Middle East, several extremist Jewish groups began a campaign against the British administration. By 1946 terrorism had invited British reprisal, and that in turn outright rebellion. Over 100,000 Jews had been illegally smuggled into Palestine since the publication of the White Paper.

In 1947 Great Britain requested that a special session of the General Assembly consider the problem. The General Assembly thereupon set up a United Nations Special Commission on Palestine, consisting of Canada, Czechoslovakia, Guatemala, India, Iran, the Netherlands, Peru, Sweden, Uruguay, and Yugoslavia. The majority report proposed partition of Palestine into Arab and Jewish states and the internationalization of Jerusalem. The minority report proposed a federal state of Palestine with two sections, Arab and Jewish. The two plans were thoroughly debated and on November 29, 1947 the General Assembly voted 33 to 13, with ten abstentions, to recommend partition. The Arab states immediately recruited volunteers who in early 1948 began to attack Jewish settlements.

Great Britain terminated its mandate on May 14, 1948 and the State of Israel came into existence on the same day— whereupon, Arab armies from Syria, Lebanon, Transjordan, Iraq, and Egypt invaded Palestine. During the conflict the great majority of Arab residents of the Jewish state fled to neighboring Arab territories. When an armistice agreement was finally signed in February of 1949 between Israel and Egypt, Lebanon, Transjordan, and Syria, Israel refused to allow the return of the refugees. These were settled near its borders in refugee camps supported by the United Nations Relief and Works Agency (UNRWA).

The presence of these refugees was a constant source of tension between Israel and the Arab states. Many of the refugees of military age were formed into guerrilla raiding units along with elements of the regular Arab armies. These units infiltrated into Israel to commit sabotage, and an accumulation of these incidents led to Israeli retaliation.

The cycle of incident and retaliation quickly became a major issue in the Security Council. On October 14–15, 1953, in response to numerous incidents on the Israeli–Jordanian border, Israeli units crossed over in the region of the village of Kibya. In the ensuing battle 53 Jordanians were killed. The Israeli–Jordanian Mixed Armistice Commission on October 15 blamed Israel for the attack.

The issue was brought before the Security Council, which on November 25, 1953, in a resolution sponsored by the United

States, Belgium, Great Britain, and France, expressed its strongest censure of that action and called upon Israel to prevent all
such actions in the future. It also called upon Jordan to prevent
all unauthorized crossing of the demarcation line. However, in
the face of continued incursions into Israeli territory by groups
of Egyptian-sponsored Fedayeen, Israel's forces on February
28, 1955 destroyed the Gaza garrison headquarters of the
Egyptian Army, killing 38 and wounding 26 Egyptians.

The Mixed Armistice Commission on March 6, 1955 accused
Israel of responsibility for the raid, and on March 29 the
Security Council, again by Western initiative, passed resolution
106 (1955) condemning the attack as a violation of Security
Council resolution 54 (1948), which had ordered an immediate
cease-fire and truce, and as inconsistent with the General
Armistice Agreement and the UN Charter. Violence continued
on the Egyptian–Israeli armistice line, violence deplored by
the Security Council in resolution 108 (1955).

As the year 1955 ended, the specter of confrontation was
shifting to the Syrian front. Continual attacks by Syrian shore
batteries on Israeli fishing vessels on Lake Tiberias precipitated
a December 11, 1955 Israeli raid on the Syrian guns emplaced
near Lake Tiberias. Forty-nine persons were killed in this
raid, and the Security Council on January 19, 1956 again issued a condemnation. Resolution 113 (1956) called upon Israel
to comply with its obligations under the Charter, threatened to
consider further measures, and recommended certain steps to
reduce tension along the borders, such as withdrawal of forces
from the armistice lines and full freedom of movement for
UN observers.

Israeli anger was provoked, however, by the continuing Fedayeen incursions as well as by Egypt's continued refusal to
allow Israeli ships access to the Gulf of Aqaba or the Suez
Canal. Egyptian acquisition of Soviet armaments heightened
the tension already manifest with the nationalization of the
Suez Canal by President Nasser in late July 1956 and the conclusion of a military agreement by Egypt, Syria, and Saudi
Arabia for a unified command under an Egyptian general. On
October 30, 1956 Israel launched an attack on Egypt and
quickly captured the Gaza Strip and the Sinai Peninsula. Great

Britain and France joined in this operation. Since the Security Council was deadlocked by British and French vetoes, the General Assembly, in a series of seven resolutions (997 [ES-1] to 1003 [ES-1]) passed from November 2–10, 1956, called for a cease-fire and the withdrawal of all troops behind the armistice lines. It also established a UN Emergency Force as a buffer between the two sides.

Israel finally withdrew to the armistice lines and the UN Emergency Force was set up in the Gaza Strip, on the armistice line, and at Sharm El-Sheikh. The attack and results discouraged any further incursions of the Fedayeen and opened the Straits of Tiran to Israeli shipping.

Security Council consideration of Middle East matters in the next few years was limited to resolution 158 (1960) on a Jordanian complaint of Israeli violation of the demilitarized zone, and resolution 162 (1961) urging Israel to comply with the decision of the Israeli-Jordanian Mixed Armistice Commission. Thus the period from 1956 (after resolution 113) to 1962 was free of Security Council condemnations.

On March 16–17, 1962, Israel attacked Syrian positions in response to repeated Syrian-sponsored incidents, and on April 9 the Security Council in resolution 171 (1962) reaffirmed its condemnation of Israeli military action in violation of the General Armistice Agreement. During the following few years Israel and Syria issued several complaints against each other but the Security Council took no action. Then on November 13, 1966, in reprisal for a series of attacks from Jordanian territory, Israel launched an attack on the village of As-Samu, an attack that the Security Council censured twelve days later, warning Israel that further steps might be taken if Israeli actions were repeated. The cycle of incident, reprisal, and condemnation had begun again.

On June 5, 1967, following the blockade of the Straits of Tiran by the United Arab Republic and the mobilization of the armed forces of Arab states in the area, war broke out. In six days Israel had won a decisive military victory and gained control of the Sinai Peninsula, the Gaza Strip, the West Bank of the Jordan River, and the Golan Heights. On June 6, 7, and 9, the Security Council called for a cease-fire, which

was finally put into effect on June 11. Continuous violations
of the cease-fire forced the Security Council to twice condemn
any and all violations, in resolution 236 on June 11 and
resolution 240 on October 25, 1967.

Since the war created many new refugees and displaced many
old ones, the Security Council in resolution 237 (1967) called
upon Israel to ensure the safety, welfare, and security of the
inhabitants of the areas now under its control as well as to
facilitate the return of those who had fled. According to the
Secretary General's report (S/8124) of August 18, 1967, more
than 100,000 Palestine refugees and 200,000 Egyptians, Jordanians, and Syrians had fled from their homes to Arab-
controlled territories. On the other hand, 550,000 of the
1,350,000 refugees fell under Israeli control.

The humiliating defeat of the Arab armies and of the Palestine Liberation Organization, and the cowardice of many of its
leaders (Ahmid Shukeiri in particular) led the refugees to believe that the only feasible way to liberate their homeland was
by waging an intensive campaign of guerrilla warfare against
Israel. To this end several guerrilla organizations gained increasing popularity, the largest being Al Fatah. These were
dedicated to the perpetration of terrorist incidents in the Israeli-
occupied territories as well as in Israel itself. At first their
major base of operations was in Jordan. Incidents multiplied
and Israeli retaliations soon became the rule. The cycle of
Arab terrorist incidents and Israeli retaliation was renewed. A
series of terrorist actions in the early months of 1968 culminated
in the Israeli attack on the Al Fatah base at Karameh on March
4, 1968, an action condemned by the Security Council in
resolution 248 on March 24, 1968. Terrorist acts continued,
and on June 4 Israeli troops attacked the village of Irbid, killing
59 Jordanians and injuring 121 others. The Security Council
was called into session the next day by complaints from Israel
and Jordan against each other. However, the news of the assas-
sination of Senator Robert Kennedy dominated the meeting, and
the complaints were not discussed. The incidents went on.

On August 4 Israel bombed the village of Salt and its out-
skirts. Jordan immediately requested a meeting to consider
"the grave situation resulting from the continued Israeli acts of

aggression against Jordan," while Israel asked for a resumption of consideration of its June 5 complaint on "the grave and continued violation of the cease-fire by Jordan." The Security Council began its deliberation on August 15.

In the debate that followed, several fundamental questions were discussed and analyzed. The essential fact of the case was agreed upon: Israel had bombed the village of Salt. Other essential questions were: Why did Israel take this action? Was the action premeditated? Was the action justified? Against whom was the action taken? Who was responsible for the entire episode? What should be done for the future?

These questions did not go far enough. The specific incident triggered other questions: What was the origin of the conflict? On whose side was justice?

In the debate itself three general positions emerged. Israel claimed that the Arabs were the aggressors and the Israeli action was based on the right of every state to defend itself. Accordingly, the Security Council should tell the Arabs to call a halt to their incessant campaign against Israel and make peace. A second position was taken by a group of states generally associated with the West—Brazil, Canada, China, Denmark, Ethiopia, France, Paraguay, the United Kingdom, and the United States—who condemned the Israeli retaliation as out of all proportion to the terrorist attack. The Israeli policy of retaliation was wrong, they said, and the Security Council should condemn it. Finally, the Arab and Communist states and their allies—Algeria, Hungary, Pakistan, Senegal, the Soviet Union, Jordan, Iraq, Saudi Arabia, Syria, and the United Arab Republic—claimed that Israel was solely responsible for the crisis and that the Security Council should employ Chapter VII of the UN Charter against it.

Since Israel openly admitted conducting the raids at Irbid and Salt the debate centered on the events preceding those attacks. The representative of Israel claimed that the attack must be considered as a reprisal for the many border and terrorist incidents that had been organized within Jordan and openly supported by that state. Israel's action was merely retaliation for these murderous assaults—an exercise in self-defense, not aggression. The Arab attacks could not be considered acts of resistance against an occupying power since the areas struck by terrorists were Israeli territory, not Israeli-occupied territory; moreover, the terrorists did not come from the Israeli-occupied West Bank but from the Jordanian East Bank. Finally, the Israeli attack was aimed at terrorist bases, not at innocent civilians. If any civilian installations were hit, it was because the Jordanians had established gun emplacements in populated areas.

The Western and pro-Western states agreed with Israel that one must include the attacks by the Arab guerrillas in any consideration of the problem, since the Israeli raids were obviously in reprisal for these attacks. It was on the second point that they differed with Israel, charging that the scale of the Israeli attack was out of proportion to the incidents that had provoked it. Whereas the Arab incursions were minor incidents, the Israeli raid had been on a major scale and therefore could not be considered pure self-defense. Such massive retaliation was unjustified in view of the provocation.

The Arab and Communist states generally followed two lines of thought. Many refused to mention any Arab attacks and insisted upon considering the Israeli attack in isolation. The Arab actions, they said, were not a relevant subject for discussion. Other Arab states discussed the Arab actions but insisted that whereas these actions were justified, Israeli acts of retaliation were not. The Arab guerrillas were merely individuals fighting to regain their land, resisting Israeli imperialist occupation. Their cause was justified; Israeli actions were aggression. In support of their case many Arab states equated the situation in the Israeli-occupied territories with that of the Nazi-occupied territories in Europe. The Arab attacks were manifestations of resistance as legitimate as the resistance to Nazi occupation in Europe.

The second Arab point followed in logical sequence. Since one should either not consider the Arab attacks at all or view them as the acts of freedom-fighters attempting to regain their homes, the Israeli action was not self-defense. Israel was the aggressor against its neighbors. In point of fact, they said, the Israelis had not attacked "terrorist bases" as they claimed but had bombed innocent villages, causing a great toll in dead and wounded civilians. This was surely aggression, not self-defense.

Although the resolution should have been limited to the particular series of incidents in the latter half of 1968, the debate soon focused on the philosophy and aims of Israel as well as on its behavior in the occupied territories.

The basic question in this regard, especially between Israel and the Arab states, was whether Israel really wanted expansion or peace. Within this question were contained several other issues, the major one being the treatment of the population in the occupied territories. Was Israel treating them humanely, or was it terrorizing and expelling the people from the area? Israel said that it had no aggressive or expansionist aims; it merely wished to live with its neighbors in peace and would withdraw from the occupied territories to agreed-upon and secure boundaries. In fact it was the Arab states who continued their belligerence and threatened to "drive Israel into the sea." Israel was in no way mistreating the Arab population in the occupied territories, and anyone who left was doing so of his own free will. Israeli acts of retaliation were not meant to humiliate its neighbors but to demonstrate its determination to defend its borders and people.

The Arab states insisted that Israel was a bastion of colonialism in the Middle East. These attacks were not for self-defense; how could a few poor Arab freedom-fighters threaten the strongest state in the Middle East? No, the attacks were meant to force Jordan to bow to Israel's dictates. By intimidating Jordan, Israel would be able to take control of that state. In addition, these attacks were intended to destroy all hopes for peace by undermining the Jarring mission, an attempt by Ambassador Gunnar Jarring to mediate between Israel and the Arab states on the basis of resolution 242 (1967) in the hope of attaining peace. Israel, they said, was a racist Jewish state that was terrorizing and expelling the peoples of the occupied territories and had no intention of withdrawing from these territories.

After each side had presented its case and Israeli intentions had been discussed, the next step was to assess responsibility. This assessment was divided into two stages. In the first, only the incident itself was considered; in the second, the entire Middle East situation. Both sought to determine the guilty party.

As to the first area of discussion, Israel insisted that the Arab states were responsible for the terrorist incidents that had led to a retaliatory raid. The Arab states, especially Egypt, had supported the raiders, given them bases in which to train, helped arm them, guided them to the areas of infiltration, and provided covering fire for them. The Arab states were responsible; they had encouraged and supported the Palestinians. States are responsible for all activities emanating from their territory.

The Arab states and their allies claimed that Israel was responsible for the guerrilla attacks. Hungary pointed out that the guerrilla raids were due to Israel's occupation of Arab lands, and Pakistan insisted that Jordan could not fight its own population in order to defend Israel. The Palestinians wished to regain their land and acted on their own, without the assistance of Arab states. Israel's retaliation was therefore illegal since the acts of individuals (the Palestinians) could in no way be equated with those of governments (Israel).

The representative of Israel claimed that general responsibility for the entire Middle East situation belonged to the Arab states. They had continually refused peace and had openly and repeatedly declared their intention of destroying Israel. They had repudiated resolution 242 of November 22, 1967, which called for Israeli withdrawal from occupied territories and the right of each state to live in peace within secure and recognized boundaries; they had waged war against Israel for twenty years; they refused to accept the very existence of Israel. This was the cause for the turmoil in the Middle East.

The Arab states contended that Israel was at the root of the problem; it had expelled the Palestinians from the homes they had lived in for hundreds of years. The Jews involved had come from Eastern Europe and forced the inhabitants to become refugees. No one could blame these peoples for attempting to return. Israel had massacred many Arabs and was mistreating its own Arabs. Israel was militarily superior so it could not feel threatened by the Arabs, yet it refused to accept Security

Council resolution 242. This demonstrated that it was an aggressive expansionist state, and the Arab states were only defending themselves against colonialism.

Having debated the facts and attempted to determine the guilt of one party, the next step was to decide what punishment to mete out.

Israel, following the line of reasoning set out above, declared that the United Nations must end Arab aggression; the Security Council must demand that the Arab states abide by the cease-fire and negotiate with Israel for a secure and durable peace. The Arab states, pursuant to their claim that Israel was the aggressor, demanded that the Security Council take the steps outlined in Chapter VII of the Charter and those mentioned in Security Council resolution 248 of March 24, 1968 which stated that the Security Council would have to consider further and more effective steps to ensure against repetition of such acts. Only in this way could Israeli aggression be stopped and peace be restored to the area.

Most other states took intermediate positions. The Soviet Union demanded a condemnation and declared its agreement in principle to further action, yet did not press too vociferously for such action. The pro-Western states demanded that all parties adhere to the cease-fire and agree to implement resolution 242. Strong support was expressed for the Jarring mission as the only way to put an end to the bloodshed. In the interim, several states suggested the stationing of more UN observers on the cease-fire lines so as to deter attacks from both sides.

Finally, the possible effects of various resolutions on the United Nations itself were considered. In Israel's view, unless the Security Council demanded that the Arabs make peace with Israel, the organization would be doing nothing to further the principles of its Charter. On the contrary, another inequitable resolution would encourage the Arab terrorist campaign of violence and unleash another cycle of bloodshed on the Middle East. Thus a resolution favoring the Arab cause would lead to war, not peace, and would lower the prestige of the United Nations in the eyes of the world.

The Arab states asserted that the Security Council must not only condemn but actually take action under Chapter VII of the Charter. The United Nations was formed to protect small and weak nations from powerful aggressors, and failure to do so in this case would demonstrate its inadequacy. Israel had flouted UN resolutions; it was time to demand compliance. Failure to protect the weak and force the aggressor to comply with its resolutions could precipitate the demise of the United Nations as it had its predecessor, the League of Nations.

Most other states thought that the UN role should be to help bring about a peaceful settlement by implementing resolution 242 through the efforts of Ambassador Jarring. Meanwhile, the United Nations could defuse the situation by stationing observers along the cease-fire lines.

Resolution 256 was adopted unanimously. Yet many states were dissatisfied with it. The Arab and Communist states and their supporters regretted that the resolution did not invoke Chapter VII of the Charter against Israel. The Western states supported the resolution but stressed their support for the Jarring mission. Israel of course objected. And the resolution demonstrated again the liabilities of the Security Council in dealing with the Mideast dispute. The distribution of members in the Security Council at this time was five Western European and North American states (Canada, Denmark, France, the United Kingdom, the United States), two Soviet bloc states (the Soviet Union, Hungary), two Latin American states (Brazil, Paraguay), three Asian states (China, India, Pakistan), and three African states (Algeria, Ethiopia, Senegal). All voted in favor of the resolution, believing that unanimity would strengthen the United Nations and perhaps have more effect than divided support.

In analyzing the incentives for condemning Israel in the Middle East crisis one must examine the relationship between the Communist states and the Arab states. The Arab states need Soviet support in the Security Council for two reasons, both dealing with a particular characteristic of the Security Council. First, the possibility exists that Arab states will not be members of the Security Council at the time of a crisis (as they were not in 1946, 1951, 1952, 1955, 1956, 1967, 1968, 1969) and therefore be unable to sponsor or present condemnatory resolutions. Second, the Afro-Asian states are a minority (40 percent)

in the Security Council and do not have the numerical strength
to pass resolutions on their own. Therefore, the support of
several other states is needed. An analysis of the sponsors of
resolutions condemning Israel reveals that the Arabs did not
actually sponsor any resolution passed by the Security Council.
Sponsors were France, the United Kingdom, and the United
States together; the United States alone; Pakistan, Mali, and
Nigeria; Senegal and Zambia; and Zambia alone. Also, India,
Pakistan, and Senegal proposed a resolution in March 1968
condemning Israel, which was not voted on by the Security
Council, and the Soviet Union has often proposed resolutions,
or pressed for strengthening others with the threat of sanctions
or expulsion. Nevertheless, the Arab states were to a large
degree responsible for the passage of the resolutions sponsored
by other states. Many were proposed by states that were allies
or sympathizers of the Arab bloc when the Arab states were
not members of the Security Council. (Until 1970, only three of
the thirteen resolutions were passed while the Arabs were
members of the Security Council.) And the sponsors of resolutions 228 through 270, Mali, Nigeria, Senegal, Zambia, and
Pakistan, have consistently voted with the Arab group and
against Israel. Of these five states, Pakistan and Mali have
never had diplomatic relations with Israel.

A second factor to be considered here is that the sponsors of
these resolutions moderated the Arab demands. Many of the
Arab-sponsored resolutions were far too drastic (for a bargain-
ing position perhaps) to have had any chance of adoption.
Thus these states sponsored compromise resolutions either because they felt that Israel had gone too far (as in the Beirut
Airport raid) or because the Arabs or the Soviet bloc had proposed an extreme resolution and the West preferred a more
moderate alternative. This was the case with resolution 111
(1956), which condemned the Israeli attack of December 11,
1955 on Syrian gun emplacements near Lake Tiberias. The
United States, the United Kingdom, and France offered it after
the Soviet Union had formally sponsored a stronger Syrian-
introduced resolution. In the case of resolution 171 (1962),
which dealt with the Israeli attack on Syrian positions on March
16–17, 1962, the United States again stood sponsor because a

far stronger Syrian-introduced resolution was being sponsored by the United Arab Republic. These Western resolutions therefore prevented the passage of far more extreme condemnations.

As in previous cases, the reasons for the strong Arab (and Soviet) pressure for condemnation of Israel can best be understood in terms of what these states hoped to accomplish. With respect to Israel itself, the Arab states pushed for the resolutions in the hope that condemnations might actually deter Israeli retaliations, which often caused extensive damage. It was a policy of defense, an attempt to create a political deterrent. As N. T. Fedorenko stated:

> Thanks to the support given them by the United States —a permanent member of the Security Council—and by certain other members of the Security Council . . . the Tel Aviv rulers were able insolently to ignore the Security Council decisions and continue and extend their aggression, overrunning more and more Arab territory.[1]

A second reason for urging the adoption of these resolutions was the Arab belief that they might create internal dissension within Israel by raising doubts as to the wisdom of Israel's policy of retaliation—perhaps even encouraging emigration from that state. There was also the possibility of causing dissension and lowering morale among Israel's military if their actions were condemned and questions were raised as to the justice of their attacks. In addition, failure to gain a political victory in spite of their obvious military superiority might discourage them.

The Arab states also hoped a series of condemnatory resolutions would make diplomatic exchanges with Israel far more difficult, and they incessantly compared Israel to the colonialist states of South Africa, Portugal, and Rhodesia as well as to Nazi-Germany in an effort to deprive the state of its friends and make it a pariah in the family of nations.

> By 1967—and this was the basic cause of Israel's aggression of June 5—we had succeeded in building up an economic situation in Jordan and most of the other Arab countries to a point where foreign investors were beginning to have serious doubts about putting money in Israel if

that meant exclusion from Arab markets. We also had isolated Israel diplomatically in wide areas of international life.[2]

Israel's prestige had risen in the international arena because of its military prowess, and the Arab states hoped a UN condemnation would serve as public affirmation that these actions were wrong and deflate Israel's reputation. At the same time, the resolutions were meant to legitimize the use of force against Israel. If the situation demanded, the Arab states could say that the United Nations, whose aim is universal peace, was obliged to sanction war against Israel in the name of self-defense against an aggressor state. Indeed, this was precisely the justification used by the Arabs for the October 1973 War—that the Arab states were implementing UN resolutions by attacking Israel.

Finally, condemnatory resolutions could help to prove the justice of Arab demands in the event of future negotiations between Israel and the Arab states and could be used to force Israel to make concessions and compromises. Nasser stated:

> All the Western countries, including the United States and Britain, speak about Israel's rights and take a partial stand. None of them speak of the Arabs and Arab rights or the rights of the Palestinians in their country and property.[3]

> The issue now at hand is not the Gulf of Aqaba, the Straits of Tiran, or the withdrawal of United Nations Emergency Forces, but the rights of the Palestinian people. . . . It is the expulsion of the Arabs from Palestine, the usurpation of their rights, and the plunder of their properties. It is the disavowal of all the United Nations resolutions in favor of the Palestinian people.[4]

With respect to other states, the first benefit to be gained from a UN condemnation of Israel would be a propaganda victory. A UN condemnation is an expression of world judgment; it would provide moral justification for the Arab position and be immensely useful as propaganda. For example, it could be used to convince the population of the Western states of the "true aims and intentions" of the Israeli government. Several prominent Arab leaders have made reference to such use:

> We want world public opinion to be on our side and really
> to know our position. . . . A major part of the battle is
> taking place on an international level and under the eyes of
> public opinion throughout the entire world, which wants to
> live in peace.[5]

> . . . realize the necessity to satisfy many parties by our solu-
> tion. For instance, if we consider world public opinion has
> some weight and influence, we must put out a solution which
> will . . . be acceptable to it, even be it with difficulty. Of
> course, when we speak about the need for satisfying world
> opinion, we do not mean in the kind of solution to the Pales-
> tine issue, but in its method.[6]

It was precisely to discourage a repetition of the events preceding the Six Day War, as described by Israel Foreign Minister
Abba Eban, that the United Nations could be used.

> Multitudes throughout the world trembled for Israel's
> fate. The single consolation lay in the surge of public opinion
> which rose up in Israel's defense. From Paris to Montevideo,
> from New York to Amsterdam, tens of thousands of per-
> sons of all ages, peoples and affiliations marched in horrified
> protest at the approaching genocide. Writers and scientists,
> religious leaders, trade union movements and even the
> Communist parties in France, Holland, Switzerland, Nor-
> way, Austria, and Finland asserted their view that Israel
> was a peace-loving state, whose peace was being wantonly
> denied. In the history of our generation it is difficult to
> think of any other hour in which progressive world opinion
> rallied in such tension and agony of spirit.[7]

The Arabs hoped that a stream of denunciations by the
United Nations might encourage Jews the world over to question
the policies of the Israeli government. Such questioning might
result in a perceptible decline in monetary contributions and
moral support, which could severely weaken Israel and make
it more amenable to compromise or even lead to its eventual
defeat. This is why Jews the world over have been an important
target of Arab propaganda. Indeed, Arab spokesmen have
tirelessly asserted that they are not against Jews per se but only
against Zionists. As Cecil A. Hourani put it, "If there is no room
in Israeli society for the Arabs, we should show that there is
room in Arab society for the Jews. . . . There are Jews . . . who

also reject the narrow vision and fanatical aims of some of their leaders, and who can be our allies. . . . Our greatest victory will be the day when the Jews in Palestine will prefer to live in an Arab society rather than in an Israeli one. It is up to us to make that possible." [8]

Finally, a condemnation of Israel would notify all parties concerned that the Arab states will not succumb to Israeli pressure and will insist on their rights. It would reaffirm the Arab position to the world at large as well as to Israel in particular. It is obvious that this determination is an important asset. Witness President Nasser's resignation broadcast at the height of the Arab defeat: "We now have several urgent tasks before us. The first is to remove the traces of this aggression against us and to stand by the Arab nation resolutely and firmly; despite the setback, the Arab nation, with all its potential and resources, is in a position to insist on the removal of the traces of the aggression." [9]

Since passage of condemnatory resolutions requires organized efforts and pressure in the United Nations, attempts to condemn Israel could have an indirect benefit for the Arab states, by forcing them to cooperate and formulate a common policy. This situation has been impossible in most other spheres, and the search for unity has been expressed by many leaders of the Arab world.

A UN condemnation of Israel would also enhance the prestige and boost the morale of the Arab guerrillas. Universal condemnation of Israel's acts against the Arab guerrillas would imply some recognition of these groups and perhaps generate increased external aid, both moral and material.

A UN condemnation of Israel could also increase Arab prestige in the world at large as well as within the Arab states. Military defeats by the Israelis serve to diminish Arab prestige. A condemnation indicates that military action may have been successful, but was morally wrong. Thus it is an attempt to salvage politically what has been lost militarily.

Finally, requests for condemnation have been in many respects an act of desperation by the Arab states, an effort to offset their people's tremendous fear of Israel. The United Nations has thus become an outlet for their emotional frustration; they want it to condemn Israel from a desire for revenge, from a feeling that something must be done to strike back at Israel. They condemn because they can do little else. "We try to act on our own when we think we are winning; we come to the United Nations when we fear we are losing. One result of this is that in our minds the international organization is associated with failures and setbacks, and rarely with successes." [10]

Along those same lines, one of the reasons for great-power sponsorship of condemnatory resolutions against Israel is to ease the tension. Emotions after an Israeli retaliatory raid are often close to the explosion point, and a condemnation is intended to accomplish two things: to give the Arabs a political victory, thereby relaxing their demands for immediate military action; and warn Israel against future attacks, thus forestalling further military action.

A great power might also press for a condemnation to strengthen the prestige of the governments of its client states in the Middle East. The Soviet Union was most concerned when the United Arab Republic or Syria was attacked, while the Western states were more concerned when Israel attacked Jordan or Lebanon. Each great power wishes to protect the government of its client state since the loss of prestige in the face of continued military blows from Israel could lead to the overthrow of that government.

A great power might also wish to demonstrate its solidarity and dependability to its client states. A public affirmation of support for its ally will aid not only the ally but the great power by increasing its prestige in the eyes of all its allies. A condemnatory resolution is a simple and inexpensive way to demonstrate support.

On the domestic front, a condemnatory resolution could serve to encourage the Arab states and their people in their struggle against Israel. Condemnation of Israel by a universal body such as the United Nations would be a clear indication to every Arab that his cause is just and that a great majority of the world population approves of the struggle.

Such action by the United Nations would serve to encourage the Arab armed forces by raising their morale (which indeed was very low when resolution 256 [1968] was under discussion). A UN condemnation might also help to increase the prestige and/or ensure the political survival of the authorities in power at the time. The prestige of a government is generally low after a military setback. (After the Six Day War, President Nasser felt compelled to offer his resignation.) The leaders of a state are held responsible for its fortunes, and a military setback weakens their position. A political victory might salvage the situation. Thus, President Nasser gained strength when the Israelis were forced to withdraw from all Egyptian territory after the 1956 war. Particularly in a case where a budding opposition is attempting to gain power, a condemnation may help the leaders of the state to retain power by diverting attention from the military defeat.

The continuing Arab struggle against Israel is conducted along all fronts: military, political, and economic; the United Nations is just one arena in this struggle. However, a condemnatory resolution represents another victory gained. And such resolutions could eventually lead to economic and military sanctions against Israel or even expulsion of that state from the United Nations—a subject much discussed in 1975. The Arab states are continually pressing for such steps and they believe that every condemnation brings them closer to this goal. In the debate on resolution 111 in December 1955 and January 1956, the representative of Syria proposed the following resolution:

> The Security Council . . .
> 4. Calls upon the Members of the United Nations to adopt the necessary measures for applying economic sanctions against Israel;
> 5. Decides to expel Israel from the United Nations Organization under Article 6 of the Charter for the persistent violation of the principles of the Charter;
> 6. Decides that Israel should pay adequate compensation for the loss and damage to life caused by the said attacks.[11]

Indeed, the General Assembly suspension of South Africa in 1974 was a hopeful sign in this direction, since the Arab states often compare Israel to South Africa.

Finally, many condemnations are passed because earlier resolutions require that any further Israeli action be condemned.

Thus resolutions seem to acquire a momentum of their own. The United Nations can neither ignore these actions nor merely deplore them since to do so would subject it to the accusation that it is retreating in the face of pressure. Yet the Western states will not allow the United Nations to take such measures as economic sanctions. Because the organization can neither withdraw nor advance, it issues another condemnation.

As to the effects of these resolutions, Israeli retaliatory raids have neither halted nor been delayed because of them. Generally, Israeli reprisals have followed increases in incidents along its border, or major raids that imperiled its security or caused many fatalities. For example, Israel immediately retaliated against Lebanon for the attack on an El Al airliner in Athens, which was a potential danger to Israeli aviation.

In fact, Israel's rejection of UN demands is evident in the history of its reprisal raids. On November 4, 1953 Israel was censured for its raid into Kibya, but in March 1954, barely four months later, it raided the Jordanian village of Nahalin. In February 1955 Israel attacked the Egyptian command in the Gaza area and inflicted heavy damage, an action that resulted in another condemnation. Yet in December of the same year it attacked Syrian positions in the Lake Tiberias area. A further condemnation for this action in 1956 failed to prevent the Suez War ten months later.

The relative calm in the next decade, 1956 to 1965, was due to a lack of incidents along the borders, not to Israeli compliance with UN directives. The UN Emergency Force prevented serious incidents along the Israeli-Egyptian border, and the Israeli-Jordanian border was relatively free of incidents except for minor disputes in the Mount Scopus area in August 1957 and May 1958. The Israeli-Syrian border was the most volatile one, suffering constant shellings and minor incidents. When these incidents became serious, Israel retaliated with an attack on Tawafiq on January 31, 1960 and another on Syrian posts in the Lake Tiberias area on March 16, 1962, for which it was again condemned.

In 1965, Al Fatah was organized with the specific purpose of harassing the Israelis. This it proceeded to do in late 1965 and 1966, forcing Israel to retaliate on September 11, 1965 against Jordan in the Qalquilaya region, on October 28, 1965 against Lebanon, and on November 12, 1966 against Jordan at As-Samu. As terrorist actions increased, so did Israeli reprisal raids.[12]

Resolution 240 of October 25, 1967 condemned all violations of the cease-fire, and resolution 248 of March 24, 1968 condemned Israel for an attack on Karameh. Nevertheless, the Israelis attacked Irbid on June 1968 and bombed Salt two months later, actions condemned by the Security Council on August 16 in resolution 256. This resolution, which warned of further measures if the attacks were not halted, was followed in less than two months by a raid on the United Arab Republic on October 31, 1968, an attack on Jordan on December 1, an air raid on northern Jordan on December 4, and the attack on Beirut Airport on December 28. In addition, barely seven months after the Security Council condemnation of the attack on the Jordanian village of Salt, Israel again bombed that area.[13] The attitude of Israel toward these resolutions was explained in Ambassador Tekoah's reply to resolution 256:

> To us in Israel this adamantly warlike posture of the Arab Governments is not a matter of Security Council debates only. . . . To us this is the continuation of the twenty-year war of Arab aggression, pursued now in particular by the method of terror warfare. . . .
> The resolution which has just been adopted . . . reminds us of the long standing disabilities under which the Security Council labours in questions arising from the Israel-Arab conflict. However, these circumstances cannot affect the fundamental precepts of law. These bestow upon Israel the inalienable right to defend itself against the continued warfare waged by the Arab states, a right enshrined in the United Nations Charter. The Government of Israel is responsible for the security of the population in Israel-controlled territory and will discharge this responsibility in accordance with its rights and duties. . . .
> Israel will do its utmost to ensure the maintenance of the cease-fire. It expects the Arab states to do the same. . . . Whatever they do . . . reciprocity remains the cornerstone of the relationship between sovereign States and it is therefore in the interests of all the peoples of the area that the cease-fire be fully respected.[14]

There were several reasons for this continual flouting of Security Council resolutions. First, in the eyes of most Israelis this was an issue of security and self-defense. Since every state has the right to defend itself, as stated in Article 51 of the UN Charter, Israel could hardly be expected to give up this right on demand, especially after the United Nations had failed to defend it on two separate occasions. Israeli leaders often re-iterated this theme of self-defense and the helplessness of the United Nations in resolving the entire Middle East dispute.

> The United Nations authorities failed to bring to the notice of the Security Council the full tale of the blood-shed in Israel. This is no case of unauthorized crossings of demarcation lines, as the draft resolution chooses to define the murderous attacks actually taking place, but a guer-rilla war, planned or tolerated by the Government of Jordan and other Arab Governments. . . . We shall take all legiti-mate measures in our power to ensure that Jewish lives too shall not be left unprotected.[15]

> So long as the Security Council has not adopted effective measures to stop the aggressor, it is the duty and the right of an attacked state to defend itself by virtue of the right reserved to every country under Article 51 of the Char-ter.[16]

Second, the failure of the Security Council to act as an im-partial arbiter in all Middle East incidents reduced its legitimacy in the eyes of many Israelis. The Soviet veto blocked any con-demnation of the Arab states in the Security Council, so Israel felt that it had no choice but to retaliate when provoked. For example, the failure of the Security Council to condemn Syria in early November 1966 may have precipitated the Israeli re-taliation against Jordan later that month. Because several com-plaints to the Security Council had failed to produce a favorable resolution, and because the Security Council was widely viewed as pro-Arab, Israel felt it had no obligation to obey the directives.

> Israel comes before a tribunal where the only alterna-tives, whatever the merits of the case, are a verdict for the Arabs or no verdict at all. . . . Would any citizen in any country seek recourse to a court where the only available

verdict was a verdict against him? In the light of what happened in the B'not Ya'acov and Suez discussions what possible weight can we attach to Syrian and Soviet contentions that if Israel had a grievance she should submit it to the Council? [17]

During the past 12 years the U.N. Security Council has never once been able to muster the unanimity necessary to censure one of Israel's neighbors, either for their incessant attacks against her security or for blatant and flagrant incitement—often uttered at the Security Council tables itself—against her sovereignty. It is bitterly ironic therefore that the Council should have saved its sharpest censure for an Israeli act of self-defense which came directly in the wake of more than 70 sabotage attacks over the past 22 months. . . .

Israel . . . cannot renounce military reprisal against aggression, if it is felt that such an action is the only way of halting border raids and safeguarding life and property here. And in this . . . Israel only reserves for itself the same rights as any other sovereign state. This is all the more compelling so long as the Security Council continues to prove itself incapable of confronting the Arab sabotage campaign which is part of an overt scheme for liquidating the State of Israel. . . .

Until the Security Council is prepared to deal with this reality, it cannot expect its appeals to be taken seriously by the Israeli public. This public has in the past 18 years well learned the lesson that Israel's own strength is the final guarantee of its security.[18]

The Israelis could not rely on the United Nations to deter the Arab attacks, so they relied on force instead—believing force to be the only language the Arabs understand. Thus, by enabling them to use force on the ground that the Security Council was not responsive to their needs, the Security Council actions may actually have been a blessing in disguise for the Israelis. If the Security Council had condemned the Arab states, Israel may have found it more difficult to justify further retaliatory raids. If the Security Council had been more objective, Israel would have been under more pressure to bring its case to the Security Council before retaliating. The fact that the Security Council was not objective in this matter gave Israel a rationale for retaliating directly without bothering to consider the Security Council as an alternative to alleviate its grievances.

Many UN delegations themselves doubted the efficacy of these condemnatory resolutions. Delegate skepticism that these resolutions would reduce the tension in the area was reported in 1966 and again in 1968.[19]

Despite the failure of Security Council resolutions to prevent Israeli retaliatory raids, they did have some effect. Israel attempted, by all means possible, to avoid these condemnations. Sometimes raids were not announced so as to prevent immediate UN condemnation.[20] At other times, Israel did not retaliate for specific provocations but bombed and raided areas as part of a minor war raging on the borders. For example, in line with its policy of "active defense" Israel launched numerous minor raids against Fatah bases with the aim of destroying the guerrilla movement either directly or indirectly, by placing pressure on the inhabitants to drive the guerrillas out. Since these acts were indistinguishable from the general border violence, it became far more difficult for the United Nations to single out specific Israeli actions to condemn.

The condemnatory resolutions also had an effect on one type of retaliatory raid. The massive world condemnation of the Beirut Airport raid in which Israel damaged or destroyed more than a dozen aircraft undoubtedly deterred Israel from further actions of this type—although it has been tempted to retaliate in this way several times since 1968. For example, on May 30, 1972, three Japanese gunmen in the employ of the Lebanon-based Popular Front for the Liberation of Palestine, killed or wounded more than 100 persons in Lod Airport, yet Israel did not undertake any direct retaliation against Lebanese civilian aviation.

The condemnatory resolutions created some minor internal dissension within Israel itself. Most Israeli citizens supported the reprisal policy in general and even pressed for reprisals for certain incidents. The *New York Times* of June 3, 1972 (p. 3) quoted Minister Galill as saying that Israel "would not rush into action in response to the pressure of public opinion impatient for a reaction."

Both the general support for the government's policies and the dissension are reflected in Israeli elections. The only large opposition bloc advocated even less compliance with UN directives than the leading government party, and after the October War, the right-wing coalition, which advocated stronger action with regard to the terrorists, had gained control of nearly one-third of the 120-member parliament.

Despite strong citizen support for retaliation, opinions were sometimes divided on specific acts, usually in the wake of a particularly severe UN censure. Some disagreed on the specific target or scope of an operation. The *New York Times* reported on December 31, 1968 (p. 1) that some Israelis were beginning to question the effectiveness of the policy of retaliation. In fact, a hard core of opposition used the Security Council condemnations as support for their arguments that reprisals were wrong and should be halted, but this was a small minority: Ha'olem Hazah and the New Communist List received 4 percent of the vote and five seats in the 1969 election and had little effect.[21] Nevertheless, budding opposition and growing doubts forced the government to continually defend its reprisal policy. Army sources reported a drop in border incidents after the December 1968 raid on Lebanon, and General Bar Lev suggested that reprisals were beginning to take effect.[22] In addition, the government asked for Knesset approval of its reprisal policy after UN condemnations—and generally received it with overwhelming majorities. In 1953 the Knesset approved the policy of retaliation by a vote of 58 to 22, in 1962 by 76 to 3, in 1968 by 61 to 3 with one abstention, and in 1969 by 70 to 1 with two abstentions.

The Israeli press was nearly unanimous in its support of government actions. Some papers questioned the wisdom of specific raids, but the government's action was strongly supported in all cases. In November 1962 the papers *Zmanim* and *Haaretz* pointed out that there was some room for self-criticism; nearly all the others strongly supported the government until the Karameh raid with its heavy Israeli casualties, when *Shearim* (March 26, 1968) called for new methods to combat Arab terrorism: "While our existence does not depend on the Security Council, we must nevertheless try to act in such a manner as not to provide too many opportunities to hypocrites and professional moralizers to incite world public opinion against us."

But even then, most newspapers continued to agree with the government. Consider the views of the following three newspapers, all published March 25, 1968: "The Security Council . . . is even now incapable of displaying an objective attitude and this is why Israel did not resort to it instead of engaging in a self-defense operation. We cannot agree . . . that there was a lack of proportion between the acts of terror and the Israeli action" (*Davar*). "We reject with loathing all the charges, full of selfish political hypocrisy, of the Arabs and Soviets at the Security Council, and their old and new satellites" (*Hayom*). "There cannot be the slightest doubt that the Defense Forces' action was one of clear self-defense, aimed at forestalling and thwarting a large-scale programme of terrorism" (*Lamerhov*).

The Security Council resolutions had no effect whatsoever in inciting military dissension. There was little disagreement in the military as to government policy.

While there was certainly some friction between Israel and its Western friends, this cannot be attributed solely to condemnations. In general, it was diverging views of national interest that determined the kind of relations Western leaders maintained with Israel. For example, relations with France cooled quickly after the 1967 war, but this was due primarily to France's desire to improve its relations with the Arab states. On the other hand, UN condemnations undoubtedly created some resentment and anger on both sides. Relations with the United Kingdom became somewhat strained, and in this case Israel's retaliation (especially against Jordan) and the subsequent Security Council condemnations did have some effect.

> The British press thought we were senseless to waste a "diplomatic achievement" we had supposedly gained following the attack on the El Al plane in Athens. These so-called diplomatic achievements are costing us much blood, for which few abroad shed tears. . . . We cannot even be shocked by the message sent from the Vatican to the President of Lebanon. . . . Does the blessing bestowed on the Lebanese people also include terrorists who kill innocent passengers on board civilian aircraft?

In 1962 Israeli leaders praised France, and in 1966 New Zealand, for their courage in abstaining on resolutions, implicitly blaming the other Western states for failing to show the same courage. In addition, Israel's relations with the United States fluctuated during all of the nearly three decades of its existence, and this may have been partially due to the reprisal raids and the subsequent condemnations.

> The reaction of the American press . . . fell back to the familiar mathematical calculations of proportions. One can cynically remind our friends across the Atlantic that the term "massive retaliation" was not invented by us. The war against Israel cannot be one-sided, and threats to damage our airliners and harm tourism cannot go unpunished.[23]

Also, a certain amount of American and British resentment has been aroused by the continuation of reprisal raids despite Security Council condemnations. Nevertheless, overall American-Israeli relations were not damaged by UN condemnations.

These resolutions did create a fear of isolation in Israel, a fear that led to a rapid program to achieve self-sufficiency. The French boycott of military goods increased this feeling of insecurity, which grew with every subsequent condemnation. Most Israelis were convinced that only the Jews cared about Israel and reliance on outside aid might be a fatal error.

The condemnations also increased the tempo and urgency of Israel's search for friends and allies. Israel launched a massive program of technical aid to many developing states. Experts were sent abroad to advise these states, and students from these states were trained in Israeli universities.

Despite these efforts, the Arab efforts to isolate Israel did bear considerable fruit after the Yom Kippur War of 1973— at least among many members of the Third World. In 1971, 35 African states maintained diplomatic relations with Israel; by 1974 most had severed these relations. Condemnatory resolutions may have helped to contribute to a sense of Third World solidarity, which was a factor in the decision of many African states to break relations with Israel in the face of the war. But probably a more crucial factor in their decision was economic pressure by the wealthy Arab states on the poverty-stricken African states. Before this war many states had maintained ex-

cellent relations with Israel even as they were voting for condemnation because of political pressures (such as Arab support
on colonial issues in return for African support against Israel).
So condemnatory resolutions could have served as a rationale
for severing relations with Israel, but were more likely a minor
factor in the decision.

The Arabs were also partially successful in diminishing
Israeli prestige, at least in the political sphere. Although the
Israelis demonstrated military prowess that gained much admira-
tion, the constant political condemnations were used in Arab
propaganda to portray Israel as an international bandit-state
acting in defiance of an impartial international organization.

The series of condemnatory resolutions did, in some respects,
legalize the use of force against Israel. While most states have
continually supported a peaceful solution of the conflict in accordance with Security Council resolution 242, the Yom Kippur
War was justified by some Arab spokesmen as a war in defense
of UN resolutions. Before that war, many Arab spokesmen
stated that they would negotiate only after Israel agreed to abide
by UN resolutions on the Middle East. In addition, resolution
242 is often cited as a reason for not negotiating directly. The
situation has changed, however, since the 1973 war, and there
is at least the possibility of negotiations; yet this is not due to
UN actions but to the results of the war. And the recognition
granted by the General Assembly to the Palestinian Liberation
Organization in 1974 may hinder and complicate the possibility
of negotiations that exist at the present time.

UN condemnations of Israel have been a major propaganda
victory for the Arab states, whose leaders have consistently
used them as proof of the immorality of the Israeli regime. However, the efficacy of this propaganda is open to question. Although the West did pressure Israel to withdraw from the
Sinai Peninsula in 1956, it has not done so since 1967. The
efforts of Secretary of State Henry Kissinger in this direction
are due more to the possibility of a renewed oil embargo and
the dangers to international peace from war in that area than
to any UN resolutions.

A study of arms sales and tourism, both reflections of the
relations between states, will best illustrate the fact that Arab

propaganda has actually had little effect in changing Western attitudes toward Israel. Although there have been rumors that the United States would cancel military contracts because of Israeli raids and subsequent UN condemnations, this has not happened. Even in 1953 when the American government halted aid to Israel, Secretary of State John Foster Dulles insisted that this was due to the Jordan River issue, not the Kibya raid.[24] Indeed, when Israel agreed to abide by the UN decision in that controversy, American aid was resumed.

In 1955 many Israelis feared that the raid on Syria would harm Sharett's plea for American arms, and Assistant Secretary Allen stated that this raid was indeed a factor in the American decision.[25] And many Israelis feared that the December 1968 Beirut raid might force cancellation of the Phantom contract and adversely influence President-elect Nixon's policies toward the Middle East. Yet the contract was not abrogated and the United States continued to supply Israel with arms despite numerous condemnations.

Tourism increased during the entire period. In 1970, 440,000 tourists visited Israel, and in 1971 this figure had increased to 650,000.[26] There was a decline in 1974, but this was due to the Yom Kippur War. This is in marked contrast to the precipitate decline in tourism to the Arab states. For example, tourism to the United Arab Republic dropped by 67 percent after the 1967 war, while the number of tourists visiting Israel skyrocketed.[27]

Another Arab objective, a decrease in Jewish support for Israel, failed to develop. Pro-Israeli demonstrations grew larger throughout the years; contributions to the United Jewish Appeal and sales of Israeli bonds rose significantly; and the American stand on condemnatory resolutions brought strong protests from the American Jewish community in 1953, in 1962, and again in 1968.[28]

> This resolution regrettably sponsored by our government failed to reflect the facts of persistent Syrian provocations, the declared Arab objective of liquidating Israel and continuous threats to the citizens of Israel and to its territorial integrity. We find almost incomprehensible this failure to distinguish between acts of aggression and self-defence.[29]

There were of course some fringe elements who strongly objected to Israel's actions and existence but the resolutions did not significantly encourage them or increase their membership and since the 1973 war these have nearly faded away and support for Israel has become nearly unanimous among American Jewry.[30]

Finally, while the resolutions did inform the world of the Arab determination to fight for its rights, as the number of condemnatory resolutions increased, there was progressively less coverage in the press, thus frustrating the Arab desire to publicize its resolve, at least until the 1973 war.

Although the resolutions did indicate some Arab unity, outside the United Nations, Arab opinions were divided—even on the subject of Israel. They ranged from the views of President Bourguiba of Tunisia, who envisioned peace with Israel at some future date, to those of Colonel Qaddafi of Libya, who fully supported the aims of the Palestinian guerrillas. In other matters the states were hopelessly deadlocked.

The resolutions did enhance the prestige and morale of the guerrillas. Some Israelis questioned the policy of retaliation for this very reason: reprisals would lead to further condemnations, which in turn would encourage the guerrillas and add to their prestige. For example, after the Israeli raid on Karameh, the *New York Times,* March 23, 1968 (p. 3) reported a rise in Arab morale.

Still, the rise and fall of Arab guerrilla prestige had far more to do with military feats and defeats than condemnations. Karameh was hailed not as a political victory but as a military one. And the guerrillas' prestige suffered a disastrous blow when they were defeated at the hands of the Jordanian Army in the civil war and consequently expelled from that state. UN condemnations were of no aid in this situation. They only contributed to the guerrilla cause in general.

The great powers that hoped these resolutions would calm the situation were sorely disappointed. The resolutions deterred neither Arab terrorism nor Israeli retaliation. In fact, they may have enlarged the scope of conflict by involving more states in the issue.

On the other hand, the resolutions clearly demonstrated

great-power support for their client states and thereby enhanced their prestige in the client states' eyes. Political support and demonstrations of solidarity were important in the Middle East and much appreciated. On the other hand, military support is far more important; it is tangible, and in itself demonstrates political support. Major General Herzog of Israel pointed out that the acquisition of Phantom jets was probably the most important event in 1969 in postponing a resurgence of hostilities; their psychological value was far more important than their military value. The Arab leaders had believed that the increase in their own strength, combined with the wear and tear on the Israeli arms and the French arms embargo, made 1969 an ideal time to launch a new strike against Israel.[31] The Israeli acquisition of the Phantoms was an immediate deterrent and implied future American military and political support.

UN condemnatory resolutions do have some effect in strengthening the client states of the great powers. The Western states pressed for the passage of resolution 228 which censured Israel for its attack on the Hebron area on November 13, 1966, so as to support King Hussein of Jordan.

> The need felt to bolster King Hussein and becalm the Jordan West Bank . . . was what led some of the nations to line up with the Arabs and the Soviet Union in backing the severe resolution. . . . But the resolution will not solve his problems any more than it will solve the problems which led Israel to mount the punitive raid in the Hebron area.[32]

The resolution was thus a substitute for military action. Yet, here again, military action and support were far more decisive than political support. It was no coincidence that while the United States was supporting a condemnation of Israel, reports circulated that the United States was carefully weighing Hussein's bid for new military aid.[33] The clear objective of these reports was to bolster the Hussein regime against the Palestinians.

On the domestic front, UN condemnatory resolutions directed against Israel encouraged the population in the Arab states, reaffirmed the justice of their beliefs, and improved their morale. The Secretary-General of the Arab League, Sd. Abdul Khaliq

Hassouna, stated on March 25, 1968 that the Security Council condemnation of Israel's attack made all Arabs look to the future with great optimism and hope.[34] Yet this encouragement was minor, and the Arab thirst for a military victory was clearly evident. Hassanian Haykal wrote:

> To my mind there is one chief method . . . in tipping the balance of fear and assurance in the Arab-Israeli conflict in favour of the Arabs. This course . . . is: to inflict a clear defeat on the Israeli Army in battle. . . .
> I am speaking . . . about a battle that is limited as battles naturally are; about a real battle, however, resulting in a clear defeat for the Israeli Army. Such a limited battle would have unlimited effects on the war.[35]

It was the realization that a military victory against Israel was not possible that encouraged the Arabs to hope for political victory as a substitute. Each condemnation was welcomed in the Arab capitals for bringing the final political victory over Israel closer; each encouraged many Arabs to believe that the great powers would repeat their intervention of 1956 and force Israel to withdraw from the occupied territories. Indeed, many Israeli spokesmen have insisted that the condemnations give the Arab states hope of gaining their ends without negotiations and without true peace.

Although UN condemnations do increase the prestige of the Arab governments in the eyes of their people, this benefit is only temporary. It soon becomes obvious that the condemnations accomplish little, and the population gradually ignores them. *Al Destour* complained on August 17, 1968 that nothing ever comes of condemnatory resolutions. On January 2, 1969 a *Baghdad News* editorial pointed out that the Security Council condemnation would be fruitless; Israel would reject it and reveal the inefficacy of Security Council decisions; the military arena determines the success or failure of governments.

In the United Nations itself, the Arab states hoped that continued condemnations of Israel would eventually lead to sanctions and/or expulsion. Arab delegates often stressed the need for sanctions because of Israel's refusal to comply with previous resolutions. In fact, this argument is often embedded in the resolutions themselves.

The Security Council . . .
1. *Deplores* the failure of Israel to abide by resolutions 262 (1968) and 270 (1969);
2. *Condemns* Israel for its premeditated military action in violation of its obligations under the Charter of the United Nations;
3. *Declares* that such armed attacks can no longer be tolerated and repeats its solemn warning to Israel that if they were to be repeated the Security Council would, in accordance with resolution 262 (1968) and the present resolution, consider taking adequate and effective steps or measures in accordance with the relevant Articles of the Charter to implement its resolutions.[36]

Although violation of previous resolutions is justification for the imposition of sanctions, the Arabs have failed to win endorsement for either sanctions or expulsion because of Western objections, at least through the end of 1975.

Nevertheless, the condemnatory resolutions have become more severe with the passage of time. The first resolutions censured the action without mentioning Israel directly, and did not threaten further action; later resolutions specifically condemned Israel's *actions;* still others (228, 262, 280) censured or condemned Israel itself, and warned that the Security Council would consider more effective measures. Eventually, however, as the resolutions were strengthened, Western support for them began to diminish. And the consistent defiance of a small but stubborn state and the monotonous round of resolutions have demonstrated the helplessness of the United Nations in this area.

For the sixth time in less than four years, the United Nations Security Council has condemned Israel for retaliatory raids against Lebanon without seriously addressing the root of the problem—deadly Palestinian guerrilla attacks against Israel from Lebanese soil. This myopic, partisan approach to incidents in the Middle East can only serve further to exacerbate tensions, to undermine the U.N.'s efforts to promote an Arab-Israeli settlement and to erode whatever confidence still exists in Security Council resolutions.[37]

However deserved was the censure meted out by the Security Council, it put the United Nations itself in a position of severe compromise and may even have set back the quest for a peaceful settlement. There was really one question why Israel was censured: not because it was guilty but because it was small and in this instance, diplomatically defenseless. . . . It was illuminating to watch the representatives of the two great powers, each of which has recently found reason to put half a million troops into a foreign country, passing stern judgment on Israel's hour-long penetration by a handful of soldiers.[38]

In summary, then, UN action in the Middle East was of minimal effectiveness. It was a propaganda victory for the Arabs but did not deter Israeli retaliatory attacks (although Israel did modify its tactics and ruled out certain types of retaliation), and it did not create serious internal dissension within Israel. It aided the Arab guerrillas, but here again, action in the military sphere was decisive. Finally, UN prestige declined because of its consistent and obviously partisan condemnations of Israel.

3

Conclusion: The Efficacy
of Condemnatory Resolutions

There are three options open to a state whose policy has been
declared illegitimate. The first, of course, is really a nonreaction
—the simple failure to react to the resolution at all. The second
option is for the state to mount a propaganda campaign defending its policy and to create or expand a foreign affairs
department that will send and brief ambassadors and other
envoys. The third is to adopt a policy that will gain the approval
of the United Nations. The reaction (or nonreaction) of the
condemned state, and that of its allies, will determine the
effectiveness of the resolution.

Parenthetically, one might consider for a moment the idea
of launching a propaganda campaign. There are, of course,
varying degrees of movement possible to a state within such a
course of action; however, if condemnation is handled as no
more than a public relations problem, its utility can be seriously
questioned. The purpose of the United Nations is, after all, to
afford states the opportunity to take action that will ensure
peace, or at least to refrain from taking action that will endanger peace and security. If the net result of condemnation is
a public relations campaign, and not a substantive effort to
change policy in a peaceful direction, then the entire concept of
collective legitimization is brought into question. If states are
simply organizing huge public relations campaigns in order to
gain collective legitimacy for their policies while their substantive actions remain unchanged, then only the procedure of
international relations is changing and not its substance at all.

Our observations with respect to public relations between
both South Africa and Israel and the other members of the

international community have indicated an increasing fear of isolation in both these states. The inhabitants as well as the governments fear that their states will become pariahs. But while there has been some domestic criticism of the controversial policies and a call for change, the dissension has been insignificant. In both states, the dissenters are only 3 or 4 percent of the electorate, as indicated by the latest elections. In South Africa, the Progressive Party, calling for a radical change in policy by incorporating blacks into the government on a one-man-one-vote basis, received 51,760 votes, or 3.43 percent of the total in the 1970 elections. Similarly, in the 1973 elections in Israel Uri Avneri and his Meri list, a small coalition of leftist peace advocates who stressed more accommodation to Arab demands, failed to gain even 1 percent of the vote and lost their seats in the Knesset. The rightist Likud opposition, advocating a hard-line against the Arabs, gained seven seats, thus controlling one-third of the parliament.

Nevertheless, both states have tried to improve their public image. Israel often sent Foreign Minister Abba Eban to Security Council debates in an attempt to forestall a condemnation. Israel also developed a large technical aid program that sent experts to many developing states to aid in their growth, and often proclaimed that it wished to aid its Arab neighbors if only the Arabs would accept.

South Africa did not attempt to prevent the passage of condemnatory resolutions in the United Nations. Instead, it often boycotted committee meetings in which South-West Africa was discussed in order to emphasize its point that the United Nations had no legal jurisdiction to discuss the case. Still, the South African Foreign Ministry periodically published short texts demonstrating the "justice and foresight" of the South African government as well as the "happiness and progress" of its Bantu inhabitants to prove that the United Nations had been misinformed when condemning South Africa. In addition, the state repeatedly offered technical and financial aid to its African neighbors in return for their cooperation. An intensive campaign was launched to convince the African leaders that they were mistaken in pressing for world condemnation of South Africa and to explain that South Africa could aid the entire continent if given the chance. When Malawi established diplomatic relations with South Africa, it was given large amounts of aid, and this fact was widely publicized in order to encourage other African states to follow its example.

The People's Republic of China made no significant effort to improve its public image abroad after the UN condemnation in 1951. Although it was not represented in the United Nations at the time of the condemnation, its allies attempted to prevent the condemnation by vigorously opposing the American-sponsored draft resolution. When the resolution was passed, the People's Republic of China denounced it, together with all other UN resolutions on the same subject. These were its only efforts to improve its public image abroad.

All three condemnatory resolutions helped to diminish the prestige of the condemned states somewhat, although military and economic events probably affected that prestige more. Resolutions did enhance the prestige of the condemning states briefly, but this soon reached a point of diminishing returns. In the South African and Israeli cases the resolutions also enhanced the prestige and morale of the guerrillas to a certain extent, although, as pointed out above, the events in the military field quickly overshadowed the effects of the condemnations. The most important effect of resolutions—from the viewpoint of the condemning states—was an international justification of their actions. American actions were justified in Korea, the African states' actions toward South Africa were declared proper, and the Arab states were told that their policy toward Israel was a correct one.

In some respects the effects of the resolutions on the policies condemned were far less favorable. All three states continued their military actions against their foes. And all three military efforts continued on the same scale as before: the People's Republic of China launched a new offensive against the UN forces; South Africa continued to mop up pockets of guerrilla resistance; Israel continued to pursue and destroy guerrillas on both sides of the border.

On the other hand, Israel and South Africa made some political moves to blunt UN criticism and made some attempt to compromise with the United Nations. South Africa instituted the policy of Bantusans in South-West Africa, a policy promising limited independence for the population of these territories. And Israel has moved to soften its policy of reprisals—by no longer announcing its raids, or by concealing them under cover of a general outbreak of fighting. However, there have been numerous reprisals under a new policy of "active defense," especially with regard to Lebanon. Yet Israel has halted some reprisals. Strong worldwide condemnation of the Beirut Airport raid in which more than a dozen civilian aircraft were damaged or destroyed has partially deterred Israel from striking again on that scale and against that type of target.

Thus both Israel and South Africa have taken or refrained from certain actions as a step toward compromise with the United Nations. South Africa still wants to annex part of South-West Africa but is willing to allow some self-rule in the other areas. Israel continues to retaliate against Arab guerrillas but disguises the raids and has ruled out certain types of targets. On the other hand, there were few political concessions by the People's Republic of China. As noted above, the state suggested its cease-fire proposal only after its May offensive had failed and another UN resolution recommended the adoption of sanctions against it.

All these resolutions were partially responsible for some increase in friction between the condemned states and their allies. The United States, the United Kingdom, and Israel antagonized South Africa by supporting the resolutions against it. The Prime Minister, members of the government, and official publications such as *South Africa Digest* often criticized these states in particular for their stand in the United Nations. Also, the United States and the United Kingdom applied some pressure on South Africa, especially by means of an arms embargo, and this angered South Africa. Leading spokesmen warned that such actions would force it to reevaluate its relations with these states, which needed protection for their shipping around the Cape. As for Israel, South Africa warned that that state could no longer count on South Africa for assistance in the event of trouble.

There was some increase in friction between Israel and its Western allies due to the policy of retaliation and the consequent UN condemnations. There were often bitter arguments between Israel and the United States, the United Kingdom, and France. Both South Africa and Israel made great efforts to gain military self-sufficiency. Both embarked on an extensive military development program and soon manufactured the bulk of their armaments locally, despite the great economic burden, because both feared that the condemnations would lead to a military embargo that would leave them defenseless.

Relations between the People's Republic of China and its allies suffered no noticeable deterioration resulting from UN condemnations. In fact, the Soviet Union probably encouraged the People's Republic of China to enter North Korea in the first place, and their relations were unlikely to suffer because of a UN condemnation.

In all three cases the major deterioration—or termination— of relations took place between the condemned state and the condemners. The Western states invoked an embargo against the People's Republic of China that hindered that state's program of extensive industrialization; the African states do not encourage trade with South Africa (although it may continue); and the Arab states have boycotted Israel. However, none of these was a result of the resolutions but preceded them—may even have been a factor in their passage. The condemnations themselves had little or no effect on the economic relations between the condemned states and their allies; in fact, trade, foreign investment, and tourism continued.

It is apparent from this that the condemnations had little or no effect on the People's Republic of China, some effect on Israel, and the most effect on South Africa, although even here the effect was not really substantial. The question is Why? Why has South Africa taken some action (however limited it may be) to pacify the United Nations, and the People's Republic of China done nothing?

Initially, it would seem that the number of condemnations is the key to their effectiveness. South Africa was condemned most often and moved farthest toward the UN position; Israel was condemned less often and was thus under less pressure to compromise; and the People's Republic of China was condemned least so it was under the least pressure. But this conclusion runs head-on into the law of diminishing returns: the more often a state is condemned the less each individual condemnation matters. This is borne out by local press coverage of the resolutions, which decreases with each condemnation.

We return now to the question of world opinion in general and the opinion of the condemned state's allies in particular. As pointed out earlier, the effectiveness of a condemnation depends upon which states support it. If the allies of a condemned state vigorously support such a resolution it will be far more effective than if a large number of its foes support it. A state's foes will obviously sponsor such a resolution; it is to its friends that a state looks for assistance and only when it fails to receive it there does it perceive danger. Since no state is self-sufficient, the pressure brought to bear by allies is often decisive.

The second factor in a resolution's effectiveness is the importance of the issue to the condemned state. Generally, the more peripheral an issue to a state's conception of its national interest, the more amenable to compromise it will be. A third consideration is the relative success of the policy being condemned. The more successful and beneficial a policy, the less a state will heed UN resolutions demanding that the policy come to a halt. A successful policy creates its own momentum as well as advocates, and a government will find it difficult to end that policy. On the other hand, a policy that has had limited success is easily discontinued.

A fourth consideration, although of far less importance than the first three, is the scope of the resolution itself. Does the resolution address itself to a specific issue or does it address itself to an entire policy? Does it demand full equality for all blacks in South Africa or merely some limited, minor rights? The more limited the resolution, the greater the chances for its implementation.

Finally, the type of reaction elicited by a resolution depends upon the type of state condemned. A resolution directed against a democratic state may elicit a greater reaction, especially with respect to propaganda, since this type of state realizes the importance of both internal and external public opinion and will try to influence it. Such a state is more prone to consider the legality of an issue and retreat somewhat when its case is

TABLE 4
Regional Voting Pattern for
Condemnatory Resolutions
498, 1805, and 256

Resolution	Eastern Europe	Western Europe/NA	Latin America	Asia	Africa
498					
People's Republic of China					
for	0	14	20	7	3
against	5	0	0	2	0
abstain	1	1	0	5	1
1805					
South Africa					
for	10	18	18	21	29
against	0	0	0	0	0
abstain	0	1	0	0	0
256					
Israel					
for	2	5	2	3	3
against	0	0	0	0	0
abstain	0	0	0	0	0

legally weak. A condemnatory resolution directed against a dictatorial state will have less chance for implementation because such a state is less concerned with public opinion and is less likely to react.

These points can be illustrated by studying the regional voting patterns for condemnatory resolutions 493, 1805, and 256.

Examining the case of the People's Republic of China in terms of the factors described in Table 4, it becomes apparent that resolution 498 would have been unlikely to elicit much reaction from that state. First, the Soviet bloc (with the exception of Yugoslavia) solidly backed Communist China both inside and outside the United Nations: it attempted to prevent the passage of any resolution or at least to limit debate to the twelve-power resolution instead of the more extreme American-sponsored resolution; and it voted against the resolution. And the Soviet Union supported the People's Republic of China on all fronts—diplomatic, economic, military, and political—probably because it encouraged the Communist Chinese to move into North Korea. Second, the resolution covered a matter that the People's Republic of China considered essential to its interests: the protection of its borders. Since the United States was the "aggressive, imperialist" enemy, an American presence at the Communist Chinese border was considered very dangerous. Many Communist Chinese leaders may have felt that this was a matter of their very survival.

Third, the resolution condemned a policy that had been very successful in that it had pushed the United States out of North Korea. Although the Communist Chinese offensive came to a halt in late January 1951, hope endured that the next offensive would defeat the UN forces. It was the failure of this offensive that made the People's Republic of China more willing to negotiate. In addition, the resolution was a broad one, calling for a general cease-fire. Since the matter was essential to the survival of the government, and since the resolution was so broad and general, the Communist Chinese decided not to obey it—especially since their allies gave them full support.

Finally, the People's Republic of China is directed by a small group of men not subject to the whims of public opinion, either external or internal. Thus, the resolution achieved little, effecting changes neither in public relations nor policy.

On the other hand, resolution 906, also directed against the People's Republic of China, did achieve success—for two basic reasons: it was clearly focused and limited in character, requesting the release of eleven American airmen, and it did not affect a policy considered essential. Of course, Secretary Dag Hammarskjöld's efforts were crucial in gaining the release of these airmen; however, the point is that the People's Republic of China decided that the gain in goodwill from a release might outweigh any gain from continued detention of the prisoners.

South Africa was in an entirely different situation. First, while the Western states did not agree to the more extreme demands of the African states, they nevertheless consented to the condemnations and did apply pressure and an arms embargo.

Thus South Africa did not have the solid support of its friends. The table shows that eighteen Western states voted in favor of resolution 1805; the only abstention was Portugal, a solid ally of South Africa at that time. Even in the debate the Western states confirmed the evils of *apartheid,* disagreeing only with the means proposed by the African states to end it.

Second, South-West Africa was not essential to the survival of South Africa. There were, of course, some who declared that if South-West Africa was conceded, South Africa itself would be next. But this was not an immediate possibility. Indeed, many Western states urged flexibility on the South-West Africa issue so as to relieve pressure on South Africa itself.

Finally, South Africa, as a pseudo-democratic state, was cognizant of the need for favorable public opinion, internally as well as externally. It was therefore willing to compromise a bit, generally along the lines recommended by the Good Offices Committee (consisting of its friends) in 1958. Had the Western states brought more pressure to bear, the South African concessions might have been greater. Evidently, most African states recognized this, since they continually requested the Western states to pressure South Africa for more concessions. For example, resolution 2325 (XXII)

> Urgently appeals to all Member states particularly the main trading partners of South Africa and those which have economic and other interests in South Africa and South-West Africa, to take effective economic and other measures designed to ensure the immediate withdrawal of the South African administration from the territory of South-West Africa.[1]

Therefore, South Africa was willing to concede and compromise up to a point necessary to satisfy its friends, although not the United Nations.

Israel has been partially receptive to UN demands, less so than South Africa but more than the People's Republic of China. As indicated above, it has not halted its policy of retaliation, changing only its tactics as to targets and timing. On the other hand, it has never again launched a retaliatory raid on the scale of the Beirut Airport raid. The Western states have drawn the line at this point; they will tolerate most reprisal raids, but not on such a scale. Thus Israel has had the tacit tolerance of its allies up to a point and will not go beyond it except in the direst emergency.

Retaliatory raids are obviously important to Israel's conception of its national interest, and they are being continued lest its security be gravely threatened. Also, many Israeli leaders believe that the reprisal policy has been fairly effective in the long run: witness the Jordanian expulsion of the guerrillas and the partial Lebanese restriction on their movements as well as the Falangist-Palestinian conflict.

Finally, as a democratic state, Israel realizes the value of public opinion, both internal and external, and has attempted to forestall UN condemnations or to counterbalance them with other public relations mechanisms outside the United Nations. For example, there was much talk about setting up a ministry of information to enhance Israel's public image.

The effectiveness of UN condemnatory resolutions, then, appears to vary directly with the degree to which it reflects world public opinion, especially the opinion of the condemned state's allies. The greater the support of the allies for a given resolution, the greater the chances for its implementation. Thus, ironically, the greater the number of allies and friends a state possesses, and the more popular a state is in the United Nations, the less amenable it will be to following UN resolutions it deems against its best interests. The pariah state, the international outlaw, is comparatively *most* cooperative with UN resolutions because it fears to alienate the few friends that remain. For example, Western support for resolutions on South-West Africa have forced South Africa to make some concessions in its policy toward that territory even if it has made few concessions in its underlying policy of *apartheid*. However, if the West were to heed the calls of African states and completely sever all relations with the pariah states, these ostracized states would then have *no* incentive for heeding UN resolutions, which would lose the partial effectiveness they now possess.

Parenthetically, the theory expounded above helps to solve a problem raised by the Yom Kippur War in the Middle East. One of the most interesting questions surfacing as a result of this war was why Israel, on the verge of victory on the Suez front, acquiesced to a cease-fire agreement. In all probability, United States pressure was crucial. But why was it so potent on this occasion?

During the war many African states broke diplomatic relations with Israel. In addition, Western European states refused to come to the aid of Israel and maintained a policy of strict neutrality—even to the extent of refusing to permit the American resupply of Israel to operate through their states. The only state willing to strongly support Israel was the United States. Such a situation led to intense Israeli bitterness toward its former allies but also to a greater fear of international isolation. Therefore, American military supplies, while essential in themselves, were far more important as a tangible expression of diplomatic and political support in a situation where Israel was growing increasingly isolated. The United States remained Israel's major ally in the international community. Israel could not afford to lose this friend and, therefore, followed American suggestions. (Obviously, U.S. pressure will be far less effective on questions of basic Israeli national security than on issues such as the October 22 cease-fire and the second Israeli-Egyptian disengagement accord, which are comparatively peripheral to its national security.)

The efficacy of condemnatory resolutions will also vary inversely with the importance of the subject matter to the condemned state, and with the success of the policy it is directed against. The more successful and popular a policy, the less the chances of the government's heeding the UN directives to end it. Thus, as long as Israeli leaders believe that retaliatory raids deter guerrilla attacks, these raids will continue despite UN protestations.

The next two principles are far less important, but nevertheless deserve some mention. The effectiveness of any resolution will vary inversely with the scope of its subject matter. The more limited the subject the greater the chances of implementation. Resolution 906 was limited and Hammarskjöld's aid saw that it succeeded. Effectiveness will also vary directly with the extent of democracy in the target state. Thus South Africa and Israel are more amenable to UN resolutions than was the People's Republic of China (even though South Africa is only a pseudo-democracy) because, relatively, the more democratic a state, the more amenable it will be to public opinion.

There seems to be near-unanimous consensus by UN officials as well as delegates of states that resolutions of collective delegitimization have little effect. Yet these resolutions clearly do have varying degrees of efficacy. Part of the problem is that by forcing states to take a position, the entire process of collective delegitimization also freezes these positions. Once a state announces its position, little room is left for maneuver. This makes change more difficult and compromise all but impossible. Changes in policy are decried by opponents as appeasement. While this clear presentation of policy is useful to the student of international affairs studying the respective positions of the states involved, it makes concessions that much more difficult. In some ways, collective delegitimization is the scholar's dream and the statesman's nightmare.

In addition to freezing the positions of all participants, collective delegitimization has an effect on the United Nations itself in its capacity for further collective delegitimizations. UN prestige drops when the organization is viewed as the instrument of a majority faction—especially in the eyes of the object state and its allies. This can be demonstrated by the present decline of support for the United Nations by Western states—for example, Congress demanding a cutback in the United States share of UN assessments and the cutoff of aid for UNESCO; the United Kingdom singularly unenthusiastic about the UN role in the Rhodesian crisis; France refusing to pay its share of the cost for UN peacekeeping activities.

In general, the position of the United Nations in a conflict affects its own legitimacy. In situations where the United Nations maintains its neutral stance, the greater its possibility for maintaining or enhancing its legitimacy not only in that conflict but in the international arena as a whole. For example, because it has remained neutral to the conflict, UN action in the Cyprus dispute has not decreased its legitimacy.

Once the United Nations deserts its neutral position in a conflict and adopts the position of one side it begins to decrease its legitimacy and authority with respect to that conflict. Thus as the United Nations moves to condemn South Africa for its policy of *apartheid* it appears to be a tool of the African states—becoming a party to the conflict instead of remaining above it. Moreover, interminable resolutions of collective delegitimization that have no perceptible effect or have too little effect to satisfy the demands of the condemning states will also diminish the legitimacy of the United Nations in the eyes of the side with which the organization has allied itself. Thus endless delegitimizations diminish UN prestige and destroy UN authority.

Unsuccessful resolutions of collective delegitimization return to haunt their creator. Each diminishes the legitimacy of the United Nations itself, weakens it, and thus contributes to a delegitimization of the United Nations even if it has no effect on the object state.

This phenomenon (the delegitimization of the United Nations itself) creates a perception of UN inefficacy which is not necessarily borne out by the facts. The unsuccessful resolutions of collective delegitimization have overshadowed the very real effects that a resolution does have when it is backed by the allies of the object state. The gap between the perception of inefficacy and the reality of varying degrees of efficacy can be accounted for by the steady decline in UN legitimacy. Even partially successful resolutions of collective delegitimization serve to strengthen this perception of inefficacy and encourage a further decline in legitimacy. It is a self-fulfilling prophecy; statesmen say that the United Nations will have little effect because its legitimacy is in question, and it therefore has little effect.

The practical efficacy of UN resolutions is also masked by a general failure to distinguish among the various types of UN resolutions. Some resolutions are only passed for their propaganda effects. For example, many condemnations of Israel are propaganda resolutions with few UN organs involved in either their passage or their implementation. On the other hand, many resolutions involve several UN organs that together attempt to create some change in the object state's policies. Resolution 906 not only condemned the People's Republic of China for not releasing the eleven imprisoned American airmen but also asked the Secretary General to take action. In this case, the resolution was effective because it utilized various UN organs in addition to the General Assembly. Similarly, in many South African cases, a number of UN organs are involved, thus increasing the chances for some success. Failure to distinguish between limited, propaganda resolutions and those actually meant to be effective (by involving other UN organs) encourages a perception of UN inefficacy.

Finally, and perhaps most important, the image of UN inefficacy has resulted from a misperception about the nature of the United Nations. The United Nations is not an independent entity, but an international arena in miniature where most international conflicts and disputes are reenacted. It is a microcosm of the larger international reality. In this institution all international conflicts—military, economic, and political—are reflected in and, to a certain extent, transferred to the political plane. The United Nations is *not* an actor on the international stage, but a microcosm of that stage.

This leads to the conclusion that there should, perhaps, be a restriction on condemnatory resolutions in general as well as other types of resolutions that are used by a majority group of states against a minority group. If the United Nations is utilized as a bludgeon by a group of states who are trying to defeat a pariah state in the political arena when they cannot do so in the military arena, then the United Nations merely becomes an extension of the military arena, an organ for the continuation of war by other means. The United Nations emerges as the scene of angry confrontations, increasing frustrations, and frozen positions that do not alleviate the conflict but may, instead, serve to intensify it.

Perhaps a more effective role for the United Nations is in another direction, that of neutral arbiter in international disputes. This is best exemplified by its role in peacekeeping operations, operations that have had a fair degree of success, at least over a limited period. Thus, UNEF did prevent serious incidents on the Egyptian-Israeli border for a decade (1957 till 1967) and the UN forces in Cyprus were relatively successful for several years. After the 1973 war, UN forces (UNEF in the Sinai Peninsula and UNDOF on the Golan Heights) were an essential element in the Separation of Forces Agreements in the

Middle East. Yet all these instances indicate a basic limitation of this type of operation; that is, they are all short-range. Each force has been effective for a certain period of time. When the problems for which these forces were meant to be a temporary solution were allowed to remain unsolved, and these forces were utilized as a substitute for peace rather than as a prelude to it, then the repressed conflict finally reached the surface and erupted into violence. Thus in 1967 UNEF was withdrawn from Egypt and the Six Day War resulted. UN forces on Cyprus prevented hostilities only until the overthrow of President Makarios and the subsequent Turkish invasion. UNEF and UNDOF are temporary expedients and if not replaced by a more permanent agreement, will be unable to prevent a fifth Arab-Israeli war.

This may indicate a future trend in UN functions. While condemnatory resolutions have not been very effective in proportion to the many resolutions passed, peacekeeping operations have had a much higher rate of success. Thus, perhaps the most effective role the United Nations can adopt in the future is as neutral arbiter of international conflicts. Indeed, the founders of the United Nations did not envision its being utilized by one major power against another in the international arena, to become merely another participant in international rivalries. This is why they instituted the great power veto in the Security Council. The United Nations must rise above conflict rather than become a partner to it. Better that the United Nations play no role at all than exacerbate a conflict by becoming an international alliance against a minority. This is all the more true at the present time when the military power envisioned by the UN founders has failed to materialize. As a partner in a conflict or a bludgeon utilized by the majority against the minority, the United Nations has little more effect than to satisfy the bruised egos of the former. It *is* effective, however, as an international actor rising above the conflict, which can be utilized by both sides as a buffer between them. Condemnatory resolutions (as well as sanctions and proposals to expel certain states for their policies) force the United Nations to become a partner to a conflict; peacekeeping operations allow it to transcend the conflict and contribute to its settlement. It is for the latter position that the United Nations is uniquely qualified and any other utilization of the organization is misuse for narrow, very often selfish ends.

The United Nations thus has clear limitations of power and function in the international arena. If these limitations are acknowledged by the majority of states and the attempt is made to work within them, the United Nations can be a successful and effective institution. If, on the other hand, crude and violent attempts are made to deny these limitations, the United Nations will gradually lose its remaining credibility and prestige. This will, paradoxically, destroy the only power base of many states in the Third World that utilize it for condemnatory resolutions.

Appendix

RESOLUTION 498 (V)
Intervention of the Central People's Government of the People's Republic of China in Korea

The General Assembly,

Noting that the Security Council, because of lack of unanimity of the permanent members, has failed to exercise its primary responsibility for the maintenance of international peace and security in regard to Chinese Communist intervention in Korea,

Noting that the Central People's Government of the People's Republic of China has not accepted United Nations proposals to bring about a cessation of hostilities in Korea with a view to peaceful settlement and that its armed forces continue their invasion of Korea and their large-scale attacks upon United Nations forces there,

1. Finds that the Central People's Government of the People's Republic of China, by giving direct aid and assistance to those who were already committing aggression in Korea and by engaging in hostilities against United Nations forces there, has itself engaged in aggression in Korea;

2. Calls upon the Central People's Government of the People's Republic of China to cause its forces and nationals in Korea to cease hostilities against the United Nations forces and to withdraw from Korea;

3. Affirms the determination of the United Nations to continue its action in Korea to meet the aggression;

4. Calls upon all States and authorities to continue to lend every assistance to the United Nations action in Korea;

5. Calls upon all States and authorities to refrain from giving any assistance to the aggressors in Korea;

6. Requests a Committee composed of the members of the Collective Measures Committee as a matter of urgency to consider additional measures to be employed to meet this aggression and to report thereon to the General Assembly, it being understood that the Committee is authorized to defer its report if the Good Offices Committee referred to in the following paragraph reports satisfactory progress in its efforts;

7. Affirms that it continues to be the policy of the United Nations to bring about a cessation of hostilities in Korea and the achievement of United Nations objectives in Korea by peaceful means, and requests the President of the General Assembly to designate forthwith two persons who would meet with him at any suitable opportunity to use their good offices to this end.

327th plenary meeting
1 February 1951

RESOLUTION 1805 (XVII)
Question of South-West Africa

The General Assembly,

Recalling its resolution 1514 (XV) of 14 December 1960 entitled "Declaration on the granting of independence to colonial countries and peoples,"

Recalling further its previous resolutions on the question of South-West Africa and in particular resolution 1702 (XVI) of 19 December 1961,

Considering its resolutions 1761 (XVII) of 6 November 1962,

Noting with appreciation the report of the Special Committee on the Situation with regard to Implementation of the Declaration on the Granting of Independence to Colonial Countries and Peoples,

Bearing in mind the findings, conclusions and recommendations set forth in two reports,

Having heard the petitioners,

Expressing its deep concern that the continuance of the critical situation in South-West Africa constitutes a serious threat to international peace and security,

1. Reaffirms its solemn proclamation of the inalienable right of the people of South-West Africa to independence and national sovereignty;

2. Condemns the continued refusal of the Government of South Africa to co-operate with the United Nations in the implementation of resolution 1702 (XVI) as well as other resolutions concerning South-West Africa;

3. Requests the Special Committee on the Situation with regard to the Implementation of the Declaration on the Granting of Independence to Colonial Countries and Peoples to discharge, *mutatis mutandis,* the tasks assigned to the Special Committee for South-West Africa by resolution 1702 (XVI), taking into consideration the special responsibilities of the United Nations with regard to the Territory of South-West Africa, and to submit to the General Assembly, at its seventeenth or eighteenth session, a report on the implementation of the present resolution;

4. Further requests all Member States to extend to the Special Committee such assistance as it may require in the discharge of these tasks;

5. Requests the Secretary-General to appoint a United Nations Technical Assistance Resident Representative for South-West Africa to achieve the objectives outlined in General Assembly resolution 1566 (XV) of 18 December 1960 and paragraph 2 (g) of resolution 1702 (XVI), in consultation with the Special Committee;

6. Requests the Secretary-General to take all necessary steps to establish an effective United Nations presence in South-West Africa;

7. Urges the Government of South Africa to refrain from:

(a) Employing direct or indirect action involving the forcible removal of indigenous inhabitants from their homes or their confinement in any particular location;

(b) Using the Territory of South-West Africa as a base for the accumulation, for internal or external purposes, of arms or armed forces;

8. Urges all Member States to take into consideration the anxieties expressed by a large number of Member States concerning the supply of arms to South Africa, and to refrain from any action likely to hinder the implementation of the present and previous General Assembly resolutions on South-West Africa;

9. Decides to maintain the question of South-West Africa on its agenda as an item requiring urgent and constant attention.

1194th plenary meeting,
14 December 1962.

RESOLUTION 256 (1968)
of 16 August 1968

The Security Council,

Having heard the statements of the representatives of Jordan and Israel,

Having noted the contents of the letters of the representative of Jordan and Israel in documents S/8616, S/8617, S/8724,

Recalling its previous resolution 248 (1968) condemning the military action launched by Israel in flagrant violation of the United Nations Charter and the cease-fire resolutions and deploring all violent incidents in violation of the cease-fire,

Considering that all violations of the cease-fire should be prevented,

Observing that both massive air attacks by Israel on Jordanian territory were of a large scale and carefully planned nature in violation of Resolution 248 (1968),

Gravely concerned about the deteriorating situation resulting therefrom,

1. Reaffirms its Resolution 248 (1968) which, *inter alia,* declares that grave violations of the cease-fire cannot be tolerated and that the Council would have to consider further and more effective steps as envisaged in the Charter to ensure against repetition of such acts;

2. Deplores the loss of life and heavy damage to property;

3. Considers that premeditated and repeated military attacks endanger the maintenance of the peace;

4. Condemns the further military attacks launched by Israel in flagrant violation of the United Nations Charter and Resolution 248 (1968) and warns that if such attacks were to be repeated the Council would duly take account of the failure to comply with the present resolution.

Adopted Unanimously at
the 1440th meeting.

Notes

1 Introduction: The Condemnatory Resolution

1. Seymour M. Lipset, *Political Man* (New York: Doubleday and Company, 1966), pp. 77–78.

2. However, an interesting trend is now developing. Many debates in the Twenty-Seventh Session of the General Assembly have focused on the issue of terrorism and the possibility of granting some type of legitimacy to national liberation movements as was eventually done with the Palestine Liberation Organization (PLO) in 1974. This leads to the possibility that the United Nations will eventually delegitimize not only the policies or actions of states but also their governments, and perhaps even the state itself in cases where national liberation movements exist.

3. Inis L. Claude, Jr., *The Changing United Nations* (New York: Random House, 1967), p. 83.

4. As a matter of fact, this passage of meaningless resolutions as well as the deliberate provocation (in some instances) of the Western states by the Afro-Asian majority may result in the delegitimization of the organization itself. A harbinger of future Western attitudes may well be found in U.S. Ambassador John Scali's remarks to the General Assembly about the "tyranny of the majority" in response to the actions of the latter on the Palestinian and South African issues in its 1974 session.

5. United Nations, General Assembly, *Resolutions adopted by the General Assembly during Its Twenty-Fifth Session,* September to December, 1970, Supplement No. 28 (New York, 1971), res. 2714 (XXV), p. 80.

6. United Nations, Security Council, *Resolutions and Decisions of the Security Council, 1969* (New York, 1970), res. 271, p. 5.

7. This is why I have placed South Africa in the nonaligned group in Tables 1 and 3.

8. See John G. Stoessinger, *The Might of Nations: World Politics in Our Time* (New York: Random House, 1961), pp. 393–407 for a good discussion of perception vs. reality in world politics.

9. John Karefa-Smart, "Africa and the United Nations," *International Organization* 19, no. 3 (Summer 1967):766.

2 Case Studies

THE PEOPLE'S REPUBLIC OF CHINA

1. United Nations, General Assembly Annexes, Fifth Session, *Supplementary Report of the Group on Cease-Fire in Korea,* A/C. 1/645, January 11, 1951 (New York: 1951), p. 13.

2. United Nations, General Assembly Annexes, Fifth Session, *Telegram, dated 17 January 1951 from the Minister for Foreign Affairs of the Central People's Government of the People's Republic of China addressed to the Acting Secretary-General for transmission to the Chairman of the First Committee of the General Assembly*, A/C. 1/653, January 17, 1951 (New York: 1951), pp. 14–15.

3. China under Chiang Kai-Shek was closely identified with the United States, while the Philippines, Thailand, and Iran were to become signatories of the CENTO and SEATO pacts in the mid-1950s.

4. "The Reminiscences of Ernest Gross" (New York: The Oral History Research Office, Columbia University, 1969), pp. 863, 921, 937, 953.

5. Leland Goodrich, *Korea: A Study of United States Policy in the United Nations* (New York: Council on Foreign Relations, 1956), p. 164.

6. United Nations, General Assembly, First Committee *Official Records*, A/C. 1/SR. 426, January 18, 1951 (New York: Fifth Session, 426th meeting, 1951), p. 502.

7. "Reminiscences of Ernest Gross," p. 982.

8. "United States Participation in the United Nations: Report by the President to the Congress for the Year 1950," Department of State Publication 4178 (Washington, D.C.: 1951), p. v.

9. Lawrence P. Weiler and Anne R. Simon, *The United States and the United Nations: The Search for International Peace and Security* (New York: Manhattan Publishing Company, 1967), p. 230.

10. Allen S. Whiting, *China Crosses the Yalu: The Decision to Enter the Korean War* (New York: The Macmillan Company, 1960), p. 166; Weiler and Simon, *U.S. and U.N.*, p. 230.

11. Whiting, *China Crosses the Yalu*, p. 166.

12. "Reminiscences of Ernest Gross," pp. 898–99.

13. Weiler and Simon, *U.S. and U.N.*, p. 268.

14. Goodrich, *Korea*, pp. 173–74.

15. Weiler and Simon, *U.S. and U.N.*, p. 250.

16. Ibid., p. 282.

17. *New York Times*, January 2, 1951, p. 22.

18. Sheldon Appleton, *The Eternal Triangle? Communist China, the United States, and the United Nations* (East Lansing, Michigan: Michigan State University Press, 1961), pp. 22, 33.

19. United Nations Charter, Chapter II, Article 4, para. 1.

20. Harold C. Hinton, *Communist China in World Politics* (Boston, Massachusetts: Houghton Mifflin Company, 1966), p. 217.

21. "Reminiscences of Ernest Gross," pp. 848, 889; Weiler and Simon, *U.S. and U.N.*, p. 278.

22. "Reminiscences of Ernest Gross," p. 933.

23. *New York Times*, February 3, 1951, p. 1.

24. Ibid., February 17, 1951, p. 3.

25. Dean Acheson, *Present at the Creation: My Years in the State Department* (New York: New American Library, 1969), pp. 661–62.

26. *The Sino-Soviet Dispute*, Keesing's Research Report (New York: Charles Scribner's Sons), pp. 1–4.

27. Edmund Clubb, *China and Russia: The Great Game* (New York: Columbia University Press, 1971), p. 321.

28. Appleton, *The Eternal Triangle?* pp. 30–31.

29. *New York Times,* February 4, 1951, Section 4, p. 1.

30. United Nations, General Assembly, *Resolutions adopted by the General Assembly during the period 16 December 1950 to 5 November 1951,* Supplement No. 20A, A/1775/Add.1 (New York: 1952), p. 2.

31. Whiting, *China Crosses the Yalu,* pp. 149–50.

32. *New York Times,* October 29, 1953, p. 1.

33. Ibid., October 30, 1953, p. 3.

34. Ibid., December 11, 1954, p. 2; December 14, 1954, p. 1.

35. Ibid., December 18, 1954, p. 1.

36. Ibid., December 19, 1954, p. 9.

37. Ibid., August 2, 1955, p. 1.

SOUTH AFRICA

1. United Nations, General Assembly Annexes, Seventeenth Session, *Official Records of the General Assembly, Seventeenth Session, Annexes, Addendum to Agenda Item 25* (New York: 1962), Chapter IX, p. 116, para. 124, document A/5238.

2. United Nations, General Assembly, *Official Records of the General Assembly, Seventeenth Session, Supplement No. 12, A/5212* (New York: 1962), p. 7.

3. Amelia C. Leiss, ed., *Apartheid and United Nations Collective Measures: An Analysis* (New York: Carnegie Endowment for International Peace, 1965), p. 1.

4. Ibid., p. 40.

5. Ibid., p. 28.

6. Victor C. Ferkiss, *Africa's Search for Identity* (New York: George Braziller, 1966), p. 141.

7. Personal interview; informant asked not to be identified.

8. Personal interview.

9. Scipio, *Emergent Africa* (New York: Simon & Schuster, 1965), p. 130.

10. Leiss, *Apartheid and UN Collective Measures,* p. 26.

11. Ibid.

12. John Karefa-Smart, "Africa and the United Nations," *International Organization* 19, no. 3 (Summer 1967):766.

13. Personal interview; informant asked not to be identified.

14. Ferkiss, *Africa's Search,* p. 214.

15. Vernon McKay, ed., *African Diplomacy: Studies in the Determinants of Foreign Policy* (New York: Fredrick A. Praeger, Publishers, 1966), p. 2.

16. Leiss, *Apartheid and UN Collective Measures,* pp. 16–17.

17. McKay, *African Diplomacy,* p. 21.

18. David A. Kay, "The Politics of Decolonization: The New Nations and the United Nations Political Process," *International Organization* 21, no. 4 (Autumn 1967):808.

19. *Cape Times,* December 15, 1961.

20. United Nations, General Assembly, *General Assembly Annex: Addendum to Agenda Item 23, Part I* (New York: 1967), pp. 195–96.

21. United Nations, General Assembly, *General Assembly Annexes: Addendum to Agenda Item 23; Twenty-First Session* (New York: 1966), p. 264.

22. Republic of South Africa, *Hansard House of Assembly Debates,* vol. 10, April 24, 1964, column 4893.

23. *South African Digest,* South African Department of Information, November 3, 1967.

24. South Africa, *Hansard House of Assembly Debates,* Third Session, Second Parliament (Cape Town: The Government Printer, 1964), 4 May to 8 May 1964, column 5540.

25. South Africa, Department of Foreign Affairs of the Republic of South Africa, *South-West Africa Survey, 1967* (Pretoria: Cape and Transvaal Printers, Ltd., 1967), p. 5.

26. South Africa, Department of Foreign Affairs of the Republic of South Africa, *Prison Administration in South Africa* (Pretoria: Cape and Transvaal Printers, Ltd., 1969), Preface.

27. South Africa, Department of Foreign Affairs of the Republic of South Africa, *Owambo* (Cape and Transvaal Printers, Ltd., 1971), Introduction.

28. Ibid., p. 37.

29. Amry Vandenbosch, *South Africa and the World: The Foreign Policy of Apartheid* (Lexington, Kentucky: University of Kentucky Press, 1968), p. 220.

30. *Hansard House of Assembly Debates,* columns 5638–41.

31. Ibid., column 5461.

32. Ibid., column 5493.

33. Ibid., column 5539.

34. Ibid., column 5506.

35. Vandenbosch, *South Africa and the World,* p. 222.

36. *South Africa Yearbook,* p. 39.

37. United Nations, General Assembly, *General Assembly Annexes: Addendum to Agenda Item 23; Twenty-Second Session* (New York: 1967), p. 183.

38. *New York Times,* July 21, 1970, p. 5.

39. Ibid., p. 1.

40. Ibid., August 3, 1964, p. 6.

41. *South Africa Yearbook,* p. 286.

42. Ibid., p. 94.

43. *Cape Times,* November 20, 1961.

44. Ibid., November 23, 1961.

45. Ibid., May 31, 1968.

46. *New York Times,* September 11, 1967, p. 4.

47. Ibid., October 13, 1970, p. 3.

48. Robert W. Peterson, ed., *South Africa and Apartheid* (New York: Facts on File, Inc., 1971), pp. 80, 96–98, 102.

49. Ibid., p. 104; Vandenbosch, *South Africa and the World,* p. 271; Peterson, *South Africa and Apartheid,* p. 109.

50. Ibid., pp. 116–17, 123–24.

51. Ibid., pp. 125–26; Vandenbosch, *South Africa and the World,* p. 257; ibid., p. 260.

52. *General Assembly Annex: Twenty-Second Session,* p. 183, para. 16, 17.

53. *Cape Times,* November 9, 1962.

54. United Nations, Security Council, Report by the Secretary-General on the Implementation of Security Council Resolution 309 (1972) con-

cerning the Question of Namibia, S/10738 (New York, 17 July 1972), p. 13.
55. United Nations, *Official Records of the General Assembly,* A/PV. 1636 (New York, 1967), p. 12.

ISRAEL

1. N. T. Fedorenko, "Perfidy and Aggression," *New Times* (Soviet weekly), June 28, 1967, quoted in Walter Laquer, ed., *The Israel-Arab Reader: A Documentary History of the Middle East* (New York: Bantam Books, 1969), p. 303.
2. Cecil A. Hourani, "The Moment of Truth: Toward a Middle East Dialogue," *Encounter* 29, no. 5 (London, 1967):3–14, quoted in Irene L. Gendzier, ed., *A Middle East Reader* (New York: Pegasus, 1969), p. 395.
3. Press Conference of President Gamal Abdel Nasser, May 29, 1967, quoted in Theodore Draper, *Israel and World Politics: Roots of the Third Arab-Israeli War* (New York: The Viking Press, 1967), pp. 230–31.
4. President Nasser's speech to members of the National Assembly, May 29, 1967, quoted in Draper, *Israel and World Politics,* p. 233.
5. President Nasser's speech at the National Congress of the Arab Socialist Union at Cairo University, July 23, 1968, quoted in Laquer, *Israel-Arab Reader,* p. 234.
6. Y. Harkabi, "Al Fatah's Doctrine," Adelphi Papers, no. 53 (December 1968) in "Fedayeen Action and Arab Strategy," Institute of Strategic Studies, London.
7. Special Session of the General Assembly, June 19, 1967, quoted in Laquer, *Israel-Arab Reader,* pp. 220–21.
8. Hourani, "The Moment of Truth," quoted in Gendzier, *A Middle East Reader,* p. 394.
9. President Nasser's Resignation Broadcast, June 9, 1967, quoted in Laquer, *Israel-Arab Reader,* p. 192.
10. Hourani, "The Moment of Truth," quoted in Gendzier, *A Middle East Reader,* p. 397.
11. United Nations, General Assembly, *Official Records of the General Assembly,* A/PV. 709 (New York, 1956), p. 9.
12. *New York Times,* September 12, 1965, section 4, p. 3; October 29, 1965, p. 7; November 13, 1966, p. 1.
13. Ibid., November 1, 1968, p. 1; December 2, 1968, p. 1; December 5, 1968, p. 1; December 29, 1968, p. 1; March 27, 1969, p. 1.
14. United Nations, Security Council, *Official Records,* S/PV. 1440 (New York, 1968), pp. 52–56.
15. Premier Ben Gurion's speech to the Knesset as reported in *Jerusalem Post,* November 23, 1953.
16. Premier Eshkol's speech to the Knesset as reported in *Jerusalem Post,* November 28, 1966.
17. Abba Eban as quoted in *Jerusalem Post,* January 17, 1956.
18. *Jerusalem Post,* November 27, 1966, editorial, p. 1.
19. *New York Times,* November 26, 1966, p. 1; March 26, 1968, p. 1.
20. Ibid., December 18, 1968, p. 11.
21. Misha Louvish and Mordechai Nurock, eds., *Facts about Israel* (Israel: Keter Publishing House, 1972), pp. 66–67.
22. *New York Times,* January 13, 1969, p. 9; January 9, 1969, p. 2.
23. Ibid., December 31, 1968, editorial, p. 1.

24. *New York Times,* October 21, 1953, p. 13.
25. Ibid., December 20, 1955, p. 17; January 16, 1956, p. 3.
26. *Facts about Israel, 1972,* p. 125.
27. *New York Times,* March 3, 1968, section 10, p. 23.
28. Ibid., November 23, 1953, p. 3; April 12, 1962, p. 26; January 2, 1969, p. 4.
29. Norman Podhoretz, "Now, Instant Zionism," in *New York Times Magazine,* Feb. 3, 1974, p. 10.
30. Conference of Presidents of Jewish Organizations, quoted in *Jerusalem Post,* April 12, 1962.
31. *New York Times,* September 14, 1969, p. 1.
32. *Jerusalem Post,* November 27, 1966, editorial, p. 1.
33. *New York Times,* November 22, 1966, p. 1.
34. *Baghdad News,* March 26, 1968.
35. Haykal, "Strategy of the War of Attrition," quoted in Laquer, *Israel-Arab Reader,* pp. 429–30.
36. United Nations, Security Council, *Official Records, Twenty-Fifth Year, Resolutions and Decisions of the Security Council, 1970* (New York: 1971), res. 280, p. 8.
37. *New York Times,* June 28, 1972, editorial.
38. *Washington Post,* January 1, 1969, editorial.

3 Conclusion: The Efficacy of Condemnatory Resolutions

1. United Nations, General Assembly, *Resolutions Adopted by the General Assembly during Its Twenty-Second Session,* September to December, 1967 (New York: 1968), vol. 1, p. 3.

Index

CPSIA information can be obtained
at www.ICGtesting.com
Printed in the USA
BVOW08s0315110118

505016BV00001B/4/P